BFI Film Classics

The BFI Film Classics is a series of books that introduces, interprets and celebrates landmarks of world cinema. Each volume offers an argument for the film's 'classic' status, together with discussion of its production and reception history, its place within a genre or national cinema, an account of its technical and aesthetic importance, and in many cases, the author's personal response to the film.

'Magnificently concentrated examples of flowing freeform critical poetry.'
Uncut

'A formidable body of work collectively generating some fascinating insights into the evolution of cinema.'
Times Higher Education Supplement

'The definitive film companion essays.'
Hotdog

'The series is a landmark in film criticism.'
Quarterly Review of Film and Video

D1210470

The lower creation I avoided, as a reflection upon our failure to attain real intellectuality. If they forced themselves on me I hated them. To put my hand on a living thing was defilement; and it made me tremble if they touched me or took too quick an interest in me. This was an atomic repulsion, like the intact course of a snowflake. The opposite would have been my choice if my head had not been tyrannous. I had a longing for the absolutism of women and animals, and lamented myself most when I saw a soldier with a girl, or a man fondling a dog, because my wish was to be as superficial, as perfected; and my jailer held me back.

T. E. Lawrence, *Seven Pillars of Wisdom*

Lawrence of Arabia

Kevin Jackson

1 · 3 - 2008
ωω
$14.95

For Robert Irwin,
Maestro di color che sanno

First published in 2007 by the
British Film Institute
21 Stephen Street, London W1T 1LN

Copyright © Kevin Jackson 2007

The British Film Institute promotes greater understanding
and appreciation of, and access to, film and moving image
culture in the UK.

British Library Cataloguing-in-Publication Data
A catalogue record for this book is available from
the British Library

ISBN 978-1-84457-178-9

Typeset by D R Bungay Associates, Burghfield, Berks

Cover design: Ashley Western
Series text design: ketchup/SE14

Printed in the UK by Cromwell Press, Trowbridge, Wiltshire

Contents

Acknowledgments   6

Introduction   7

1 Lawrence and *Lawrence*   13

2 1919–39   26

3 1945–61   40

4 Shoot Part One: Jordan   56

5 Shoot Part Two: Spain, Morocco, England   75

6 Release and Reactions: 1962   94

7 Reputation and Restoration: 1962–2007   107

Notes   119

Credits   123

Select Bibliography   126

Acknowledgments

My greatest debt is to Adrian Turner, both for his generous and civil encouragement by phone and e-mail, and for his admirable, pioneering works *The Making of 'Lawrence of Arabia'* (1994) and *Robert Bolt: Scenes from Two Lives* (1998). I hope that at least some of those who read this essay will go on to hunt down *Making*, a book as sumptuous as it is hard to find. My debt to Kevin Brownlow's work will be apparent to anyone who has read his definitive biography of David Lean.

I would also like to thank: Rebecca Barden of the BFI for commissioning the book, and Sarah Watt for caretaking it during her leave; Richard Cohen for sage advice; Ben Cuddon for hospitality and research efforts in Cairo; Robert Irwin for bibliographies and general wisdom; Claire Preston for eliminating many infelicities of style; Martin Wallen for Lawrentian enthusiasm; Zahid Warley for books and encouragement; and particular thanks to TC, a late but more than welcome contributor of verbal advice and visual wisdom. All lapses of taste and intelligence are mine alone.

Introduction

I long for people to look down on me and despise me, and I'm too shy to take the filthy steps which would publicly shame me, and put me into their contempt. I want to dirty myself outwardly, so that my person may properly reflect the dirtiness which it conceals … and I shrink from dirtying the outside, while I've eaten, avidly eaten, every filthy morsel which chance threw in my way.

T. E. Lawrence to Mrs Charlotte Shaw, 28 September 1925[1]

This short book changed species in the writing, and again in the editing (when I chopped more than 10,000 words). I had originally intended to offer what was mainly a rhapsodic evocation of the film, duly leavened with material both from its production history and from odd corners of the life and mythos of T. E. Lawrence – a figure who has fascinated me since well before I first saw David Lean's film. In fact, it was a BBC production of Terence Rattigan's play *Ross* 1960 (see below), and that adolescent classic *The Outsider* (1956), by Colin Wilson, which brought me the recognition that Lawrence was not at all the swashbuckling action hero of received schoolboy wisdom. Every keen student of Lawrence finds or creates a particular identity for the man; thanks in part to these encounters, my personal Lawrence has belonged more obviously with Rimbaud, Kafka and Wittgenstein

T. E. Lawrence by Howard Coster, 1931

than with Nelson or Wellington. By the time I saw the movie, I was
more than ready to relish its hero's neurasthenic agonies; even in my
teenage callowness I could sense that the film was pensive as well as
exciting and nakedly rapturous.

My plans for the essay were derailed by reading Adrian Turner's
excellent book *The Making of 'Lawrence of Arabia'*. At first glance,
this handsome volume looked likely to free me, as I'd hoped, to
concentrate almost wholly on playing Walter Pater. It tells the story
of *Lawrence*'s production history with as much thoroughness and
clarity as anyone could wish; and I congratulated Mr Turner on this
when he kindly agreed to discuss the film. But there were
complications. The book is out of print; the company which
published it has gone out of business; and the plates have been
destroyed, so there is no possibility of a reprint. It is now so rare, Mr
Turner went on, that old copies are being sold for several hundred
pounds. (This was too modest: at my last check on ABE, it was being
offered for $1500.) For most practical purposes, it no longer exists.

The scarcity of Adrian Turner's book imposed a different set of
obligations; as did my awareness that, in the decade or so since it was
published, a good deal more work has been done on the history of
attempts to bring Lawrence's exploits to the screen from the 1920s
onwards – notably in a study edited by Andrew Kelly *et al.*, *Filming
T. E. Lawrence: Korda's Lost Epics* (1997). And my readings in
Lawrence's correspondence, as well as some recent biographies,
showed that his attitude to the cinema was (as usual) far more
complicated than one might gather from his frequently cited phrase 'I
loathe the notion of being celluloided.'

It also became clear that at least some of the virtues I wanted to
highlight in the film might well be brought out by documenting the
financial, logistical, political and personal background to its
production – including, where possible, the ways in which the
completed movie often recapitulates elements from its long evolution.
Miles Malleson's 1938 version of the script, for instance, contains
several scenes which are strikingly close to the Bolt–Wilson screenplay.

Lean and Bolt were quite right in their insistence that anything that smacked of cowboys-and-indians antics, or of the *Desert Song*, should be ruthlessly expunged from their work, but they were not unique in such scrupulousness: Leslie Howard, a strong candidate for the part of Lawrence decades earlier, had reached the same conclusions.

With only limited space available in the BFI series format, a sacrifice had to be made; and, deciding that Paterian eulogies would no doubt be a good deal more enjoyable for the writer than the reader, I opted mainly for narrative and documentation rather than dissection and evocation. I hope, though, that the details I have brought into the foreground will often imply, or even state, the brilliance of the hundreds of inventions which, massed together, give the film the weight of a masterpiece: O'Toole's improvised business with his dagger, John Box's dressing of the 'mirage' sequence, Lean's bold orchestration of the attack on Aqaba ...

That the film is worthy of the term 'masterpiece' is a truth more often acknowledged by film-makers and filmgoers than by critics. In popular polls, it usually comes somewhere near the top of Greatest British Films, and almost as high on lists of the Greatest Films Ever. Critics seldom agree.[2] This is nothing new: Lean distrusted intellectuals, whom he regarded as a whining, sordid crew, and intellectuals have frequently reciprocated. (How curious that Lean's greatest film should take for its subject a scholar, poet and *homme de lettres* who had cause to lament the hypertrophy of his own intellect.) With a few admirable exceptions, critics have tended either to dismiss Lean's entire body of work as vacuous, middle-brow spectacle-mongering, or to lavish praise on his early British films – particularly the Dickens adaptations – the better to disdain his international productions.

Taking a cue from Lawrence as strategist – and Lawrence himself (who, though it often suited him to pretend otherwise, was saturated in military history from his boyhood on) claimed the deep inspiration of Belisarius,[3] one of his most potent ego ideals – I have decided to attack this climate of advanced opinion in a series of

small-scale nuisance raids rather than by means of frontal assault. Lest my war aims be mistaken, though, I should state unequivocally that I consider *Lawrence of Arabia* not just a remarkable and uniquely moving work, but one of the films which has vindicated the medium of cinema even as it expanded its possibilities.

It is certainly not a flawless piece. The style(s) of acting are often larger and more theatrical than those to which we have become accustomed since 1962; the cod-biblical style of Bolt's Arab dialogue can sound a little corny; we no longer find it so easy to accept non-Arab actors in Arab roles; Lawrence's quivering self-pity is given too much rein in the later scenes; the distortions of history and politics – as I will outline below – sometimes cross the line from dramatic licence to near-libel. And so on. Homer, in short, nods.

What I would contend is that the film's larger achievement is of a scale which renders most of these blemishes nugatory. Many viewers have sensed something mystical implicit in the film – a mysticism that comes closest to the surface in the scenes which follow Lawrence's fated journey from Aqaba to Cairo, and realism gives way to hallucination and dream. This seems a just intuition, and by its very nature not susceptible to any critical ploy more searching than the invitation to agree or dissent – though the mystic qualities must surely owe something to the simple experience of living in the desert, a trial and a privilege which awed all but the most phlegmatic crew members.

There is a comparable (perhaps kindred) quality of the recondite about the film's unique brilliance – not hard to evoke, almost impossible to explain. One can contend that it is Lean's best (his only truly great?) film, as it is Spiegel's; Bolt's best screenplay (Spielberg thinks it the best ever); O'Toole's best performance, and Sharif's; Young's best camerawork; Jarre's best score … a dazzling confluence, yet the film is bigger even than the sum of these admirable parts. I cannot presume to say why this is so, but the following chapters are a modest attempt to describe how it is so.

KJ

1 Lawrence and *Lawrence*

I do not often confess it to people, but I am always aware that madness lies very near me, always.

TE to H. S. Ede, 3 January 1935[4]

Titles and Names

There are incomparable splendours in store, quite soon, yet the film's overture is simple to the point of self-effacement: a single, static overhead shot of a middle-aged man preparing to ride his motorcycle. If it were not for the grand landscape format of the image, and a luminous, almost golden glow that suffuses it, we might be watching something quite dour and drab and social-realist. The orchestral score, meanwhile, soars and strains, in a manner we would find incongruous to the point of bathos if we did not know, or could not guess, that it is less a direct accompaniment of this mundane sight than a promise of stirring matter ahead. Then the written credits corroborate what most of us already know: this movie is *Lawrence of Arabia*, and our motorcyclist must be Lawrence of Arabia himself.

Or is he? A pedant might say no. 'Lawrence' himself might have said no, angrily ... As we soon discover, the character played by Peter O'Toole is about to take his fatal motorbike ride; the date must therefore be 13 May 1935, and on that day the man with the bike went by the legal name of Mr T. E. Shaw; his friends usually called him 'TE', and that seems to have pleased him best. ... (TE died in hospital, never having regained consciousness, on 19 May.) Until very recently, before his retirement from the Royal Air Force at the age of forty-six, he had officially been A/c 1 338171 Shaw, T. E., and was a stickler for using his service number. Noël Coward made an affectionate joke about it, in a letter that began 'Dear 338171 (May I call you 338?) …'.[5]

Names have weight, and the small man who bore the name 'Lawrence of Arabia' often did so as one might bear an uncomfortable, at times an agonising, burden. He tried everything he could to shed that name and all the myths it conjured up, including brutal renunciations of everything he cherished, from the life of the mind to bodily privacy. Spurning all attempts to make him into a grand public man, he enlisted pseudonymously in the ranks, where he tried for a while to become a complete automaton: 'mind-suicide' was one of his terms for this grand refusal.[6] One way of telling TE's life story would be as a kind of quest for his 'true' name.

His father was called Chapman – 'Chapman of Arabia' does not quite have the proper lilt – but adopted the family name 'Lawrence' when he left his wife and went to live with the woman who would bear him five illegitimate children, including Thomas Edward – 'Ned' or 'Neddy' – on 16 August 1888. (16 August, as TE liked to remember, was also Napoleon's birthday.) TE would always sign letters to his mother as 'Ned' or simply 'N', and in his later years he seems to have toyed with the idea of resurrecting the 'Chapman'. Had he done so, he would have been the second Chapman in English literary history to have translated Homer's *Odyssey*.[7]

During World War I, 2nd Lt Lawrence (subsequently Captain, Major, Lt Colonel and ultimately Colonel Lawrence) became known to his Arab comrades as 'Aurens' or 'Lurens' or 'Runs' or more wittily as 'Emir Dynamit': King Dynamite. It was the American showman Lowell Thomas who created the 'Lawrence of Arabia' name and cult – Thomas also referred to him as the 'White King of the Arabs' – and when TE fled from this glamorous legend into the RAF, he became 352087 A/c 2 John Hume Ross, until an officer discovered and betrayed him. John Hume Ross remained the name on his cheque books for the rest of his life, and he used it as the *nom de plume* for his translation of *Le Gigantesque*, a novel about a redwood tree.

He took the name 'Shaw' in 1927 – not, he said, with any thought of his good friend George Bernard Shaw, nor his even closer friend Mrs Charlotte Shaw, the playwright's wife, though some have doubted his denials. He served in the Tank Corps for three years as 7875698 Trooper Shaw, T. E. Thanks to his passion for Brough motorbikes, he became known to his fellow rankers as 'Broughie' Shaw. In his role as a writer, he used various pseudonyms, including 'CD' or 'Colin Dale' (after the underground station Colindale, the last he had used before his departure to Karachi, where he served from 1927–9). When he wanted to book a room at the Union Jack Club, he used the trusty adulterer's standby of 'Smith' – 353172 A/c Smith.

Aircraftman Shaw at
RAF Miranshah, 1928

Ezra Pound addressed him, with heavy jocularity, as 'Hadji ben Abt el Bakshish, Prince de Meque, Two-Sworded Samurai'.[8] Sir Ronald Storrs called him 'the Uncrowned King of Arabia', and after his death the Turkish press, no friends to his reputation, called him 'King of the Desert' – metaphors, to be sure, but with some grounding in fact. His noble friend Prince Feisal awarded him the honorary title 'Prince of Mecca'.

And so on. What are we to make of this? It does not require great psychological penetration to guess that a man who chafes and fidgets against the confines of a single, definitive name is likely to be complex, restless. Troubled?

Identity and Reality

Very little of that biographical information finds its way directly into the film.[9] Yet the screenwriter, Robert Bolt, was well versed in the Lawrentian lore and well aware of what it implied for his task: '... of course the whole story of Lawrence is a man trying to find an identity for himself – Aircraftsman Shaw, Sheik this, Colonel Lawrence of the secret service.'[10]

Lean's most self-consciously surreal effect – the ship in the desert

Just so: and Bolt's screenplay for *Lawrence* turns again and again to the vexed question of who Lawrence might be. In this regard, one of its key scenes – a strange, trance-like sequence which owes much to pictorial surrealism[11] – is the moment when Lawrence, almost at the end of his tether, finally reaches the Suez Canal after his disastrous crossing of the Sinai desert. A British serviceman calls out: 'Who are you?' (The line, interesting to note, was dubbed by David Lean.) Almost every sequence of the film proposes a subtly different answer to that question.

Who was he? On the positive side, Lawrence is shown as brave, stoical, visionary, tenacious, chivalric and innovative: a brilliant military strategist, a man quite free of the stupid racism of his brother officers (who cheerily call their Arab allies 'wogs') and of their antiquated notions of warfare; a scholar and aesthete; a superb linguist[12]; a compassionate man who hates injustice and sneers at pomp; a humble and exact participant observer of Arab societies who can quote the Holy Qu'ran by heart. On the negative: insubordinate, gauche, scruffy, sarcastic, narcissistic, foppish, silly, gullible, overweeningly arrogant, capricious and, in the long run, murderous – the instigator of and willing participant in an appalling massacre. Above all, Bolt's Lawrence seethes with neuroses.

Given this intense complexity, one of the things that is truly remarkable about Bolt's screenplay is how very tight-lipped it is on the subject of its hero's 'back story' – or its 'forward story': all that the uninitiated viewer will know about Lawrence's fate after Arabia is that he will ultimately die in a motorcycle accident. We learn from Lawrence's encounter with Murray that he is 'well educated'; from a fireside chat with his guide Tafas that he is 'different' from his fellow countrymen; from a similar nocturnal talk with Sherif Ali that he is the bastard son of 'Sir Thomas Chapman' … and that is about all.

Earlier versions of the screenplay, by other hands, had begun with Lawrence as an undergraduate at Oxford, or as an excavator on the British Museum site at Carchemish on the Euphrates. Biographies often begin with the powerful influence of TE's mother, and the fundamentalist religious atmosphere in which he was raised. The average present-day screenwriting tutor might call Bolt's elisions sloppy workmanship, but given the nature of its hero – initially a stranger to himself, as well as to the audience – it is entirely apt. Bolt's Lawrence is a vivid psychological portrait, but the film has requirements greater than mere portraiture. It is epic, and tragic, not only biographical.

Epic: a sustained poetic narrative about the birth or fate of nations. Tragedy: the genre of an outstanding individual, a hero, destroyed by some fatal flaw. We do not need to know what Hamlet studied at Wittenberg; we do not need to know that Lawrence – a Hamlet forced to play the part of an Achilles – had once been a mediaeval historian, a dreamer over troubadour poetry, a connoisseur of crusader architecture and a follower of William Morris. The film is at once scathing about myth in its modern sense – the wilful

Peter O'Toole holding a copy of *Seven Pillars of Wisdom* in front of Augustus John's well-known portrait of Lawrence

fabrication of useful illusions for mass consumption – and a potent instance of mythological narrative in the traditional sense. Bolt, though a fine playwright, is plainly no Shakespeare (the language of his script is admirably terse, intelligent and well crafted, but it seldom aspires to poetry); but his dramaturgical methods here can fairly be called Shakespearean. He constructs convincing but larger-than-life, quasi-legendary characters from a hint or two in the chronicles; he uses those characters to represent forces, ideologies, philosophies as well as mere personalities. Shakespeare, however, would have killed his man in Act V, not Act I.

Bolt's work is also Shakespearean in its haughty disregard for historical fidelity. His primary source is TE's own account of the Arab Revolt, *Seven Pillars of Wisdom*, which means that his view of the conflict is necessarily partial; and though he stays true to the broad sweep of TE's narrative, he seldom scruples to change events and characters when there is dramatic potential to be exploited. The character of 'Gasim', for instance, is a conflation of two different men: one whom Lawrence saved in the desert, one whom he had to kill to mediate a potentially ruinous tribal conflict. By making one man of the two, Bolt offers a stinging blow to Lawrence's faith in himself as a Nietszchean superman. (Islamic viewers might also regard the episode as an instructive parable for blasphemers: 'Ah, so it was written'.)

Does this high-handed way with facts damage the film beyond redemption, make it nothing better than an irresponsible fantasy? The question is thornier than, say, with the *Henry IV* plays, since many of those who took part in the conflict were still alive, or only very recently dead, when the film was released in 1962; and some of the political consequences of Lawrence's campaign persist into the twenty-first century. There are moments when Bolt's script enters that treacherous zone which lies between licence and libel. At one extreme, there is his representation of the taking of Aqaba, the exultant high point of the film's first half. TE's conquest of the city was indeed a victory, but a much more anti-climactic one than the

film's: the Royal Navy had shelled the town into ruins, Turkish morale was all but crushed and the mass surrender to TE's troops took place, on 6 July 1917, on the hills outside town. Hardly a shot was fired.

Now, an accurate account of this battle would be extremely dull. Besides, the film needs forcefully and thrillingly to show its audience something that can only truly be appreciated by generals or military historians: that TE was a strategist of genius. The scene, in short, is true in spirit to TE's accomplishments, however false in letter. Contrast the film's view of the taking of Damascus. Of his own account, TE admitted: 'I was on thin ice when I wrote the Damascus

Lawrence's own photograph of the attack on Aqaba, 6 July 1917 chapter, and anyone who copies me will be through it, if he is not careful.'[13] Lean and Bolt took the plunge. They make it seem as if the Arab forces were the first liberators of the city, and virtually write out the essential contributions of British, Indian and Anzac forces, in a manner understandably offensive to those who knew the reality. Indeed, the film as a whole minimises the presence of any British forces in TE's campaigns, though the first appendix to *Seven Pillars* provides a long roll-call of those British troops who served in the Hejaz Armoured Car Company and the Ten-Pounder Talbot Battery.[14]

When the film opened, it met with howls of indignation from injured parties, notably from TE's young brother Professor A. W. Lawrence, who fiercely denied that TE could have taken any active part in the notorious massacre of a retreating Turkish column – the moral low-water mark of the film's hero. There have been other such protests, from assorted political perspectives, and some are worthy of serious consideration.

Only the starchiest precisian would deny, however, that the liberties which make *Lawrence* preposterously unreliable history generally add to its potency as drama. (One possible exception is Bolt's decision to make Lawrence unaware of the Sykes–Picot treaty, a secret agreement between France and Britain as to the post-war fate of the Arab territories which made all their promises of independence hollow. TE's awareness of this treaty was, and remained, one of his deepest sources of torment.) We do not read *The Iliad* for an exact history of the Trojan War, or the *Morte d'Arthur* – TE's constant companion in the desert[15] – for a true portrait of the Once and Future King.

Bolt, an anti-imperialist and pacifist from childhood on, had been raised in the belief that generals of the Lawrence class were scoundrels. To make Lawrence sympathetic to himself as well as to audiences – and both he and Lean confessed to coming round to a far more sympathetic view of TE by the end of production – he had to draw up a fairly crude moral scheme, in which the Arabs are, if hot-headed and prickly, almost wholly virtuous, the Turks almost wholly wicked, and the British almost wholly duplicitous or, at best, lethally pragmatic. (Lawrence aside, the leading British characters are: Murray, a pig-headed dinosaur; Dryden, a sly and serpentine worker in the shadows; Brighton, a well-intentioned dimwit. Only Allenby preserves his dignity, though his offended family did not think so: Bolt's Allenby is an honourable and intelligent man obliged by duty and patriotism to enforce a dishonourable policy.) Lawrence, a naif as well as a genius, is tempted and corrupted by all three factions.

The death of the hero

Shaw/Lawrence sets off on his fatal ride. (We are in Dorset, by the way. Our hero has been living in his Spartan cottage, Clouds Hill. Carved above the door was a motto from Herodotus: *Ou Phrontis*: 'Does Not Care'.[16] He is off to send a telegram to his friend, the writer Henry Williamson, who not long since had been trying to recruit TE to the cause of British Fascism. TE had turned him down

Lawrence's cottage at Clouds Hill, Dorset

with a light quip.) An ascetic throughout his life – TE often said, and was not lying, that his favourite meal was bread and water – he found his main sensuous pleasure in speed. Going too fast as usual, he swerves to avoid boys on bicycles, loses control, crashes. In 1935, many people thought that TE had been assassinated. Many others murmured that the whole thing had been staged, and that Lawrence had been smuggled away on a secret mission, perhaps for the government, perhaps for the Fascists. (Similar rumours later attached

Lawrence on one of his Brough Superior motorcycles

Lawrence in Damascus,
2 October 1918

themselves to Elvis Presley and Jim Morrison, secular gods of a different kind.) Those who knew his dark side – and he had seriously threatened suicide at least once in the past – wondered whether it might not have been a willed accident, a drastic resolution to the problem of what to do with his life now that he was an old man of forty-six and the RAF had used him up.[17]

Lean cuts from the cyclist's goggles hanging on a twig to St Paul's Cathedral – the great national memorial service. As in the 'March of Time' sequence near the beginning of *Citizen Kane* (1941)[18], the scene appears to propose Lawrence as an enigma the film's main narrative will solve. We meet characters who will later become familiar to us: Brighton, Allenby, the American journalist Bentley and others, each of whom expresses some trenchant or evasive opinion about the man. Instead of citing the script, here are some conflicting real-life verdicts on TE:

Sir Winston Churchill: 'One of the greatest beings alive in our
time.'[19]
Allenby: 'I had several officers who would have done as well and
some who would have done better.'[20]
Major-General Rankin: '… this little tinpot fake swaggering around
taking whatever kudos was coming.'[21]
John Buchan: '… I am not much of a hero-worshipper, but I think I
could have followed him over the edge of the world.'[22]

'Chips' Channon: 'He had none of a gentleman's instincts.'[23]

Lawrence Durrell: '... a tedious adolescent applying the thumbscrews of denial to himself. Yes, a sort of nasty child. ...'[24]

Lowell Thomas (in 1962): 'After forty-five years, do I still think that one day he may be another Achilles, Siegfried, or El Cid? Yes, I do.'[25]

C. S. Jarvis: 'Lawrence was a great man and ... will go down in posterity as the finest guerilla commander that has ever existed ... it is no exaggeration to say that only a superman could have achieved what he did.'[26]

A. E. Chambers: 'He was one of the finest men who've ever trod the globe, better than Christ or any of them. He hated injustice.'[27]

One measure of *Lawrence of Arabia*'s achievement is that, by the end of its three and a half hours of running time, it manages gracefully and plausibly to encompass all of these perspectives, and others.

2 1919–39

I was very conscious of the bundled powers and entities within me; it was their character which hid. There was my craving to be liked – so strong and nervous that never could I open myself friendly to another … There was a craving to be famous; and a horror of being known to like being known. Contempt for my passion for distinction made me refuse every offered honour …

TE, *Seven Pillars of Wisdom*

Miss Garbo sounds a really sympathetic woman! The poor soul. I feel for her.

TE to Lady Astor, 31 December 1933[28]

It has often been said that 'Lawrence of Arabia' was created by the cinema: meaning not only that TE was a fairly obscure figure before Lowell Thomas's travelling movie show made him into a hero, but that Thomas's entertainment established the basic terms of the myth: Lawrence the modern-day crusader, the David who toppled the Ottoman Goliath. In broad strokes, this view of Thomas's influence is quite true; so that the elements of ambiguity, satire and horror in the Lean–Bolt treatment can be seen as principled demythologising – as a corrective to his simple adventure yarn. For more than four decades, assorted film-makers attempted to make a full-length feature about Lawrence; in retrospect, we can be grateful for their failures, since it is unlikely that any film made much before the mid-1950s, however intelligent, could have embraced such profound disenchantment.

The full story of Lawrence and the moving picture begins long before his death. TE can be glimpsed in the background of the official newsreel *Allenby's Entry into Jerusalem*, released in March 1918; not much in the way of a screen début. But Lowell Thomas was soon to change all that. On 14 August 1919, he came to the Royal Opera House, Covent Garden, to present an illustrated lecture, 'With Allenby in Palestine' – soon to be renamed 'With Allenby in Palestine and Lawrence in Arabia' when it became apparent which soldier was the more appealing.

Born in Colorado in 1892, Thomas had been something of a drifter and a roughneck, working as a cowboy and a miner before landing a job on a Chicago newspaper. In 1914 he re-invented himself as a documentary film-maker. He went to Europe to cover the fighting in France, Belgium and Italy, then asked permission to join Allenby. The Foreign Office agreed, and Thomas found himself the only film-maker with access to Lawrence and his Arabian forces. Thomas's show was horribly corny – it included a dance of the seven veils! – but hugely effective. Rightly horrified by what they were beginning to learn of the trench war, the British public was hungry

The Strand Magazine, January 1920

for gallantry, for moral clarity: in a word, for a war hero. Thomas's Lawrence fit the bill perfectly.[29]

The show ran for six months. By the early months of 1920, the title 'Lawrence in Arabia' had been taken up by the general public and modified to Lawrence OF Arabia. A full-length film treatment seemed inevitable; oddly, there is evidence that the first move in this direction was made by TE himself.

In his autobiography *Twenty-Five Thousand Sunsets* – written, it should be noted, many years after the event, in 1967, and in convalescence from a serious illness – the British producer Herbert Wilcox recalled being visited by TE and his literary agent Raymond Savage (the year, unspecified, would probably have been around 1926) with the proposal for a film version of *Revolt in the Desert*. Wilcox remembers that

In a hesitant voice, which became stronger and deeper as he went along, the author gave me an outline of his book which I found extremely interesting but not good cinema and in spots rather sordid …

I ventured the opinion that I could not see cinema audiences being attracted to such a subject. Lawrence did not agree – neither did Savage. Lawrence told me that one day it would make an outstanding film. He failed to sway me – but how right he was.[30]

Did this episode really happen as Wilcox recalled it? If so, TE must have undergone a profound change of opinion not very long afterwards, since his correspondence of the next eight years echoes with attempts to fend off directors and producers. In 1927, Rex Ingram – incidentally, a great inspiration for the young David Lean, and one of the private subscribers to *Seven Pillars* – seems to have made a tactful approach, which was no less tactfully rejected:

I do not envy you your film job. It must be a very difficult art, an expression of yourself (and of the author of the scenario) at two removes. Indeed I wonder that it is ever so good as it seems to be. They babble sometimes to me of making a film of *Revolt in the Desert*. I have no property in it so I hope they will not. Hollywood offered £6,000 or something, which the trustees turned down. Long may they go on turning it down. I'd hate to see myself parodied on the pitiful basis of my record of what the fellows with me did.[31]

Ingram took the hint. Next, in 1929, the English producer M. A. Wetherell, tried unsuccessfully to buy the film rights for *Revolt*: TE's correspondence for the next few months is full of glum references to the film industry, but by the end of the year, the project was dead. The capitalist world would have to wait for a while; the communist world did not. It is a bizarre footnote to the Lawrence saga that the first fully dramatised account of Lawrence to reach the screen was a Soviet production, *Visitor from Mecca*, first shown in Moscow cinemas in 1930. The film's hero is an engineer, working on a rail tunnel to link Russia and 'Gulistan' (Afghanistan?), whose labours are blocked by the dastardly machinations of the British Resident, in alliance with an Islamic holy man. The Resident thus stands for imperialism, and the holy man for religious reaction. Our young hero triumphs: the Resident is assassinated and the holy man shown to be Lawrence, disguised behind a false beard.[32]

TE's next appearance as a fictional character was on the English stage. On 1 September 1932 he travelled to Malvern for the first night of a new play by Shaw, *Too True to Be Good*. TE is affectionately parodied in the second act as 'Private Meek', a soldier who always knows more than his commanding officer about what is going on. The play was then staged in both Birmingham and London, where TE went backstage to thank Walter Hudd, who played Meek, 'for making the part neither impudent nor servile (its dangers) and tried to hide my regret that the counterfeit was so much nicer than the original.'[33] Hudd himself wrote of TE: 'His most striking characteristic appeared to be his *repose*. This aspect of him I had already used, however. He spoke briefly and quietly, examined me curiously, and then shyly withdrew.'[34]

Korda

For most of the next decade, the story of Lawrence and the cinema is dominated by Alexander Korda, who seems to have become interested in the project early in 1934. In late April 1934 TE heard from one of the trustees of *Revolt* that there were new plans to make a film.[35] The news plunged him into one of his frequent depressions.

TE to the Hon. Edward Eliot, 24 May 1934:

A splurge in the *Daily Mail*, talking of a film to be made around my squalid past. I wonder how much of it is true? The article talked glibly of the *Seven Pillars*; so I imagine it is mostly the perfervid imagining of one of the horde of publicity men who afflict the film world ... Tell your film negotiators that I'll be a very awkward pebble in the rock of their progress![36]

TE to Robin Buxton, 7 June 1934: 'Savage [TE's agent] is a nuisance with his film-greediness; but I suspect that Korda will not play. I am too recent to make a good subject – too much alive, in fact ...'[37]

By August, though, he had given in. TE to Robin Buxton, 14 August 1934:

Well, if they want to film the rotten book, they must. Will you please try and arrange for the scenario to be shown you ... and for me to see it, before it is used? ...

As for the actor to play me ... well, Walter Hudd was magnificent ... but perhaps Leslie Howard might be more unlike, which would be an advantage![38]

TE to Mrs Charlotte Shaw, 16 November 1934: 'The film is going to fall through, I think: a relief, for the film world only lives by publicity.'[39]

In the course of that year, TE had also become worried that an American version of his life might be made. He feared the worst: vulgarisation, bogus 'love interest'. It may have been largely for this reason that he compromised with Korda; at any rate, the contract with Korda specified that 'no female characters' were to be introduced. Korda announced that the film would be directed by Lewis Milestone – who had made the celebrated pacifist film about World War I, *All Quiet on the Western Front* – and with Leslie Howard in the lead. Korda also had discussions with the military historian Captain Basil Liddell Hart, TE's biographer and friend.

But TE developed cold feet and asked Korda to postpone. To his surprise, Korda agreed: TE to Mrs Charlotte Shaw, 26 January 1935: '… it will not be done. You can imagine how much this gladdens me.'[40]

TE told his friends the Sims family that the only film he could have borne to be made about his campaign would have been a Disney cartoon in the manner of *Three Little Pigs* or *The Grasshopper and the Ant*: 'Me and my army jogging across a skyline on camels could have been very amusing.'[41]

TE to Robert Graves, 4 February 1935:

I loathe the notion of being celluloided. My rare visits to cinemas always deepen in me a sense of their superficial falsity … vulgarity, I would have said, only I like the vulgarity that means common man, and the badness of films seems to me like an edited and below-the-belt speciousness. Yet the news-theatres, as they call them (little cinemas here and there that present fact, photographed and current fact only) delight me. The camera seems wholly in place as journalism: but when it tries to re-create it boobs and puts my teeth on edge. So there won't be a film of me.[42]

Post mortem

TE's accidental death changed everything, though Korda maintained that his position was firm:

Colonel Lawrence was the greatest personality I have ever met. If his relatives or his friends object to the film being made, it will never be made by me and no-one else will be allowed to make it. I could never contemplate such a thing.[43]

The men who might have played Lawrence
(clockwise from above): Walter Hudd, Leslie
Howard, Clifford Evans, Laurence Olivier,
Cary Grant and John Clements

Ace Films commemorated, or exploited, TE's death with a thirty-six-minute documentary, *Lawrence of Arabia*, based mainly on stills from the Imperial War Museum. Lawrence's trustees now gave Korda the go-ahead for the deferred production; and much of his energy for the next four years was squandered on the attempt to bring TE to the screen. One of his first moves was to hire Colonel Stirling – lately military adviser to King Zog of Albania – as military adviser.

In January 1936, Korda announced that *Revolt in the Desert* would be going into production in the coming year. Zoltán Korda, his brother, director of the 'imperial' trilogy of *Sanders of the River* (1935), *The Drum* (1938) and *The Four Feathers* (1939), would be taking over from Lewis Milestone. To write the script, he recruited John Monk Saunders, a World War I combat pilot, who had written a number of aerial action pictures (*The Eagle and the Hawk*, *Wings*, *Ace of Aces*) and had won the 1930 Academy Award for *The Dawn Patrol*. Walter Hudd would be Lawrence and Raymond Massey was offered the role of Feisal. Saunders's script was approved by the trustees on 29 December 1936. But political realities stood in the way of creation: Palestine was in chaos – a General Strike, terrorist attacks, assassinations. By the time a semblance of order had returned, Korda's team had been dispersed and a new one formed. Saunders was replaced as writer by Miles Malleson, the actor and playwright.[44]

Korda signed Brian Desmond Hurst as the new director; Hurst was a Northern Irishman who could speak Arabic. In partnership with Duncan Guthrie, Hurst set about preparing a shooting script from Malleson's text. Meanwhile, Korda had rejected Hudd and was busy screen-testing other possible leads. His first choice for the role was John Clements, but he soon changed his mind and announced his intention to cast, by turn, Clifford Evans, Robert Donat, Leslie Howard (again) and Laurence Olivier. All of this activity fizzled out when Korda cancelled Hurst's location trip to Jerusalem. The Palestinian government had forbidden large gatherings of Arabs, and without crowds of Arab extras the film was unthinkable.

Korda then sold the project to New World Films, based at Denham. New World nominated Harold Schuster as director and the outstanding Chinese-American cameraman James Wong Howe as cinematographer. But New World found it impossible to come up with a satisfactory script. Korda bought back the rights of *Revolt in the Desert* in the summer of 1937, returned to the Malleson draft and renamed the project *Lawrence of Arabia*. In October 1937, he announced that Leslie Howard (yet again) was to play the lead, with William K. Howard directing. On 20 November, Leslie Howard gave a lengthy interview to *Film Weekly* – 'How I Shall Play Lawrence' – explaining his approach to the film. It is in many ways an admirable exposition of the hazards and riches of the subject, and suggests that the Korda epic would have shunned vulgarities:

The picture must be free altogether of the Bengal Lancer aspect; it must have nothing Kiplingesque or sentimental; above all, it must have no shrieking Arabs riding across the desert in the manner of cowboys …

Bill Howard is the ideal person for the job [of director]. His American films … show that he can penetrate beyond the superficial actions of his characters and show an audience what is going on in their minds. I think that he is capable of capturing the drama and the mysticism of Lawrence's Arabian adventure …

Howard goes on to say that he has discussed Lawrence's character at some length with Winston Churchill, and has become persuaded that Lawrence is 'a truly tragic figure … a poet with great powers of perception'. Quoting at length from *Seven Pillars*, he speaks of Lawrence's attempt to live exactly like the Arabs and to share their privations; and of the deep loneliness that resulted, when Lawrence discovered that he no longer thought as a Westerner but could never genuinely become an Arab. Howard hopes that he will be able to convey this dimension of the character by using soliloquies – the film must be more than 'a mere adventure story':

I want to avoid that above all else. I should like the picture, as it progresses, to take on the shape of a tragedy: the ultimate defeat of all Lawrence's ideals by the well-meaning, uncompromising machine of British government ...

A great climactic scene would show Lawrence confronted by the Arab leaders, who greet him with angry silence, convinced that he had betrayed them.

Resentful and powerless to alter the decision of the government, Lawrence returns home to do his great penance.

In the final sequence I hope to show him riding to his death along a country lane on his powerful motorcycle. Then some sort of quick shot back to Palestine with its intrigues and insurrections – a tormented stretch of land which, if only Lawrence had had his way, might by now be a peaceful and united country.[45]

It was announced that a second unit had been despatched to Egypt to shoot locations, since the continuing disturbances in Palestine made it unsafe. At this point, Korda was faced with yet another political problem: the one which would finally put paid to his ambitions. Following standard policy when dealing with 'friendly foreign countries', London Films sent a copy of the script to the Turkish Embassy, asking if there were any objections to its depiction of Turkish people and institutions. There were indeed. On 25 October, the counsellor at the Turkish Embassy, Mr Ors, went to the Foreign Office to protest to G. W. Rendell. In the film, according to Rendell, he said that '... the Turks were represented as tyrants and oppressors of Arabs, and he felt it was most undesirable that a film which cast such aspersions on Turkish history and national character should be exhibited.'[46]

This complaint left Rendell in something of a quandary, especially as he was not entirely sure whether this London Films production was the same as the New World film or a wholly distinct project. It is not hard to sense his irritation with the whole business in his summing-up: '... I suppose that in present international conditions we cannot afford to quarrel with any potential friends, and we must therefore do our best'.[47]

His main practical suggestion was a polite consultation with Sir Edward Villers at New World. By 1 December, Villers had informed them that he was no longer connected with *Revolt in the Desert*, since it had reverted to Korda, but that he still knew Korda and could have a word with him.

The issue rumbled on. Korda's determination to make the film persisted well into 1938: when Zoltán Korda was shooting *The Four Feathers* in Egypt and the Sudan, Alexander sent the crew a cable ordering them to stay on and shoot exteriors for use in *Lawrence of Arabia*. But those scenes were never shot, and the *Four Feathers* unit returned to England. Its star, John Clements, asked Korda why they had not proceeded as planned. Korda's reply strongly suggests that he had finally caved in to pressure from the Foreign Office: 'How can I make a film of *Lawrence of Arabia*? We are friendly with the Turks.'[48]

Korda next sold the project as a package to Paramount Film Services, the British subsidiary of Paramount Pictures. This looked like quite a coup for Paramount, since there had been a good deal of interest in the Lawrence saga throughout Hollywood, and both Metro-Goldwyn-Mayer and Universal had registered the title *Lawrence of Arabia* in 1937. But Paramount Film Services soon found themselves confronting the same forms of resistance that had worn Korda down.

On 17 October 1938, Paramount submitted their script to the British Board of Film Censors. Its first reader was a Colonel Hanna, who poured cold water. '… It may not be prohibitive to exhibit a film of this nature at this time but I venture to say emphatically that it would be most impolitic.'[49] The script was forwarded to the Foreign Office (FO), where it was read by several interested parties. The general conclusion was that the Turkish government would have entirely legitimate grounds for complaint were the film to be produced in its present form. One of the readers noted that

It is true that the episode of history with which the film deals was a defeat for the Turks, but it seems hardly necessary, for that reason, that the Turks should invariably be painted – as is the case – in the blackest colours and shown in the most disparaging and humiliating light.[50]

A proposed list of cuts and changes were considered by Lord Tyrrell and others. At a meeting of the British Board of Film Censors on 3 November 1938, 'eventually it was decided that it would be advisable not to hold out any hope to the producers that the film, if produced, would be certificated.' Paramount Film Services dropped the project almost immediately. Once again, Korda bought back the project rights, and approached Columbia Pictures. Cary Grant was now proposed as the new star; but Columbia, scenting Korda's precarious finances, also withdrew.

Korda made one final stab at the project in May 1939. He approached the FO to ask if their line on the film's unsuitability had in any way softened. Acting as the soul of moderation, he stressed that he was eager to collaborate with the FO's chosen representatives. The FO offered mild – very mild – encouragement. Korda began to meet and correspond with Sir Robert Vansittart. A letter he wrote to Vansittart on 26 June 1939 offers a glimpse of the sort of film he now had in mind – something very far removed from the simple adaptation of *Revolt in the Desert* which he had first envisaged:

My associates and myself are fully convinced that the making of a film about Lawrence's life is today very greatly in the National Interest, as nothing could have such good propaganda effect as the example of his life.

This company is appreciative of the delicacy of the Turkish problem, and has therefore decided that the picture it is going to make about Lawrence will be based on the following lines:

– about 5 per cent of the picture will be played at Oxford showing Lawrence's life there and his departure for Arabia;

– the second part of the picture, consisting of roughly 45 per cent of the whole film, will be the War Period, in which we will take great care to show the Turks as heroic opponents and to avoid any scenes which would be detrimental to the Turkish people.

I hope that the rest of the picture will present no difficulties at all, as we will deal in passing with Lawrence's work in connection with Versailles Peace Treaty. We will then carry on to the period of Lawrence's life showing the beginning of the Royal Air Force.

This is by far the most important part of the picture we are planning, and we hope that by showing this unique climax to his life we will make the film more complete and more interesting than if we only concentrated on his exploits in Arabia during the war. By dealing so shortly with the Arabian chapter of Lawrence's life, I feel that our problems regarding any doubts of the Foreign Office will be dealt with much more easily.[51]

Vansittart congratulated Korda on this new approach: 'most satisfactory'. But nothing came of it. A few months later, Britain was at war with Germany. (Where, strange to relate, the cinema industry was busy with their own Lawrentian project. Dr Goebbels's propaganda department produced a film entitled *Uprising in Damascus*, in which Lawrence, the arch-villain, is depicted as a cunning agent of British Imperialism and Zionism. The 1930s are thus book-ended by Soviet and Nazi attacks on TE.) Korda departed for Hollywood. His rights to the Lawrence material expired in 1945, and he made no attempts to renew them.

3 1945–61

True there lurked always that Will uneasily waiting to burst out. My brain was sudden and silent as a wild cat, my senses like mud clogging its feet, and my self (conscious always of itself and its shyness) telling the beast it was bad form to spring and vulgar to feed upon the kill. So meshed in nerves and hesitation, it could not be a thing to be afraid of; yet it was a real beast, and this book its mangy skin, dried, stuffed, and set up squarely for men to stare at.

TE, *Seven Pillars of Wisdom*

After a post-war lull, the race to bring Lawrence's exploits to the screen began again. Korda's elapsed rights to *Revolt in the Desert* were taken up by an Italian production company, Ortus. Robin Maugham, the nephew of the novelist W. Somerset Maugham, was commissioned to write a script, but the project broke down when A. W. Lawrence demanded full script approval, and refused to allow an American actor to play Lawrence. The Turkish government also disapproved. Again, the rights lapsed.

On St Valentine's Day, 1951, a Jordanian producer, Michel Talhami, bought the rights to *Revolt* for £3,000 for his company Nomad Productions. Talhami took the project to Columbia, where Harry Cohn was interested. By 22 October 1951, a script – in Arabic, by the Egyptian writer Habib Jamati – had been completed and translated into English. Talhami wanted Laurence Olivier for the lead, but his hopes were soon dashed. Olivier wrote to Storrs:

It may seem a dreadful thing to say about the story of your greatest friend, but the honest fact is that much as one may admire him and hold him in everlasting homage, I simply do not feel myself drawn towards making this subject ... I just cannot *feel* it.[52]

Meanwhile, Columbia pushed ahead with the search for a suitable director. The first choice was unlikely: the team of Frank Launder and Sidney Gilliatt, noted for their literate melodramas and comedies. 'The Archers', a.k.a. Michael Powell and Emeric Pressburger, were also approached. (An Archers *Lawrence* might have been a thing of wonder; though vastly different from Lean's: more dreamlike and high-fantastical, perhaps.) But they passed. Harry Cohn was interested in David Lean, who was under contract to Korda, had just completed *The Sound Barrier* and was hunting around for a new project.

Adrian Turner found a revealing fragment of correspondence in the Columbia files:

> May 2 1952
> Dear Harry Cohn
> This is to tell you how excited I am by the Lawrence of Arabia idea ... I can't think of a better subject for my first film in America.
> Best wishes, David Lean[53]

At almost exactly the same time, the American-backed *Lawrence* proposal was matched by an English one. Terence Rattigan, the successful West End playwright, had long been fascinated by the Lawrence tale, particularly by what he saw as its homosexual themes and the enigma of Lawrence's 'mind-suicide'. Rattigan had gone into partnership with the producer Anatole De Grunwald; to complicate matters, there were rumours that De Grunwald had also established a clandestine partnership with Talhami. De Grunwald soon bowed out, but Rattigan stayed on, since Columbia had by now rejected Jamati's script and were in pressing need of a new one. Rattigan was now the obvious candidate. Lean, too, approved of Rattigan, and suggested that they should make a research trip to the Middle East in the summer, and collaborate on the script in the autumn of 1952, so as to be ready for a shoot in the spring of 1953.

Yet barely two weeks after his first letter to Cohn, on 16 May 1952, Lean quit the project. His main reason was financial: he was facing big alimony demands. He duly departed for Venice to direct *Summertime* (1955) for Korda. Without Lean as director, Columbia's enthusiasm for the project ebbed, not least because A. W. Lawrence was unbending in his opposition. He had read the Rattigan script and disapproved of its open hints that Lawrence was queer. Rattigan, himself discreetly gay, was tenacious. In 1955 he went back to work, and produced a screenplay which began and ended at the air force station described in *The Mint*, thus book-ending a stylised account of the Arabian campaigns. For Rattigan, the central event, and the key to Lawrence's later renunciations, was his rape at Deraa, which had awakened him to his true sexual identity.

Rattigan approached the aristocratic (and gay) director Anthony Asquith. Once again, De Grunwald came out of the shadows and was appointed producer. The Rank Organisation set a budget of $700,000 and stated that their film would be shot both in Pinewood and on location in Iraq. *Lawrence of Arabia* would star Britain's most popular juvenile lead of the day, Dirk Bogarde. This time, a force even more decisive than A. W. Lawrence intervened: there was a revolution in Iraq.

1956: Lawrence the outsider

The publication in 1956 of Colin Wilson's study *The Outsider* did a great deal to reshape the Lawrence myth among the reading public. Wilson, a self-educated working-class man in his middle twenties, chose Lawrence as one of the leading figures in his pantheon of nineteenth- and twentieth-century visionaries, rebels, mystics and nay-sayers. The Wilson Lawrence was a spiritual brother of Dostoevsky, Nietzsche and Van Gogh: part saint, part *Übermensch*. 'His most characteristic trait is his inability to *stop thinking*. Thought imprisons him; it is an unending misery, because he knows the meaning of freedom.'[54] Wilson's book was lauded in the Sundays by the likes of Cyril Connolly and Philip Toynbee, who then turned on him when they discovered that he was not quite the tractable prodigy they had hoped. Today, Wilson's work could hardly be more unfashionable. It seems only fair, then, to point out that his portrait of Lawrence is in many ways quite astute: recall that Dostoevsky, Nietzsche and Melville were TE's three main points of aspiration when he wrote *Seven Pillars*. There is no record that Bolt read *The Outsider*, but the Lawrence of Bolt's script and that of Wilson's book are strikingly similar.

Enter Spiegel

It was not until 1959 that a producer with both the skills and the tenacity for the task applied himself to the Lawrence myth: the remarkable Sam Spiegel. Born in 1901 (or possibly 1903: the shady elements of Spiegel's career begin with his birth) in a Polish region of

Sam Spiegel on location

the Austro-Hungarian empire, the young Spiegel managed to escape death in a pogrom, attended the University of Vienna, and arrived in Palestine in the early 1920s. In 1927 he made his way to Hollywood, whence he was sent back to Europe to supervise German and French versions of American productions in Berlin. He narrowly escaped death for a second time in 1933, when he fled Nazi Germany for London.

There, he managed to persuade a gullible millionaire to back a film called *The Invader* (1935), starring Buster Keaton. The film went down in a flurry of bouncing cheques, and Spiegel served a prison term for fraud. Changing his name to S. P. Eagle, he smuggled himself back into the United States. Many found him ridiculous, but he managed to make a powerful friend in Harry Cohn, and began to produce some serious films, including Orson Welles's *The Stranger* (1946). By 1948 had joined forces with John Huston to found Horizon Pictures.

The great breakthrough came in 1951, when Spiegel and Huston made *The African Queen* – a critical and commercial hit. Spiegel went on to produce *On the Waterfront* (1954), and, rightly sensing that it would be a landmark film, re-adopted his true name. He moved to London, and looked around for a new project. It was Carl Foreman, a blacklisted screenwriter, who brought him the option for a novel by Pierre Boulle, *The Bridge on the River Kwai*. Eventually, Spiegel decided to work with a director who, he believed, would not chafe under a strong producer: David Lean.

Lean

David Lean was born into a middle-class Quaker family in 1908, and suffered a grimly boring childhood in the suburbs of South London. His parents were moralising and pious – though his father abandoned the family for another woman in 1923 – and the young David was a poor scholar. He had one great passion – taking photographs with his Box Brownie. Forbidden to visit the cinema, he went anyway, and discovered a vocation. He joined Gaumont Film Studios in 1927, at nineteen, and served a long apprenticeship as dogsbody, until he finally landed a job in the cutting room. For the first time in his life, he excelled, and by the mid-1930s was acknowledged as the best film editor in Britain.

The next step came when Noël Coward hired Lean as co-director of *In Which We Serve* (1942). Lean proved a natural, so Coward hired him to direct his next three films – *This Happy Breed* (1943), *Blithe Spirit* and *Brief Encounter* (both 1945), a film which made him the first British director to achieve an Academy Award nomination. Striking out on his own, Lean then made two distinguished Dickens adaptations: *Great Expectations* (1946, also nominated for an Oscar), and *Oliver Twist* (1948). By the mid-1950s Lean was widely regarded as the leading director in the British cinema – a title challenged only by Carol Reed. But that cinema was entering one of its many periods of decline, and Lean hungered for higher achievements. Spiegel was a godsend.

Kwai

Lean admired Pierre Boulle's novel, but thought that Foreman's screenplay was unusable. Spiegel, Lean and Foreman put their heads together. Foreman wrote three drafts, then took off for a research trip to Ceylon (Sri Lanka). Here, he heard that Lean still hated the script. After various complicated to-ings and fro-ings, Foreman surrendered, and suggested that Lean might like to finish working on the script with a friend of his, another blacklisted American writer, Michael Wilson.

Wilson flew to Ceylon from Paris and spent an intensive six weeks polishing the Foreman–Lean script. Lean declared himself satisfied, the film went into production, and, on its release in November 1957, became a worldwide success. It had cost $2.8 million, and by 1980 its worldwide gross was over $22 million, which made it the twenty-third top-earning film to date. Spiegel bought himself a Park Avenue penthouse and a five-hundred-ton yacht, the *Malahne*. Lean was deluged with offers.

The one shadow was the question of screen credit. When Oscar time came around, *Kwai* took seven awards, including 'Best Screenplay' by ... Pierre Boulle. (Boulle himself was always happy to admit that he had not written so much as a line of the script.) Word soon got out that *Kwai* was actually the work of Foreman and Wilson, but nothing was done to change the bogus credit. Wilson's protests were soothed by an attractive new offer. Spiegel commissioned him to write *Lawrence of Arabia*.

Before tackling the script itself, Wilson hammered out a document entitled 'Elements and Facets of the Theme', dated 20 September 1959. His political hostility to Lawrence is manifest:

In trying to serve two masters, Lawrence betrayed them both. Part of Lawrence's tragedy was his intellectualism. With his inheritance of western culture, he could never really hope to submerge himself in an alien culture. Did he not serve to introduce into the Arab world the very evils from which he had fled? ... He was a man who, fleeing blindly from a deadly disease to a healthy land, himself afflicts it with the plague.[55]

Marlon Brando, 1959

Not, one would have thought, the sweetest of music to A. W.'s ears. Yet when Wilson went on to write a first treatment, A. W. declared himself so impressed that he wrote back immediately granting Spiegel the rights to *Seven Pillars*. The participants – Spiegel, Lean, Professor Lawrence and Mr G. Wren-Howard of Jonathan Cape – met on 11 February 1960. Spiegel asked the unworldly Lawrence if he had a sum in mind. Lawrence had not, so Spiegel proposed £22,500. 'Done!' said Lawrence, who no doubt considered this a handsome sum. His publisher had wanted him to demand £100,000. The initial payment to Lawrence would be £17,500; the remainder would be held in reserve. The contract stated that if Lawrence refused to grant Horizon Pictures the use of the title *Seven Pillars of Wisdom* within four weeks of the receipt of a final script, it would revert to the film company.

Less than a week later, on 17 February 1960, Columbia Pictures held a press conference at Claridge's in London to announce the next Sam Spiegel/David Lean production: *Seven Pillars of Wisdom*, with Marlon Brando as T. E. Lawrence. The choice was, to put it mildly, surprising, and one of the journalists wittily asked if Brando's were a speaking role? – since he was already notorious for his mumbling.

Rattigan was piqued at having his pet subject snatched away. He decided to address Lawrence in another medium, and announced that he had signed a contract with Captain Basil Liddell Hart, permitting the use of his biography of T. E. for a stage play to be entitled *Ross*. A. W. Lawrence attempted to block the production, but Rattigan out-manoeuvred him by saying that if the play were banned in the West End he would have it produced on television instead.

Ross opened at the Theatre Royal, Haymarket, on 12 May 1960, with Alec Guinness in the lead role. Reviews were enthusiastic, and the box office brisk.

Spiegel, disturbed by this rival activity, was still more worried to learn that Herbert Wilcox – the producer who claimed to have spurned TE's approaches – had bought rights to the stage play, and planned to start shooting the film of *Ross* in March 1961 with Laurence Harvey as star. Lean, meanwhile, had still not proposed a date for the start of his production. Spiegel threatened litigation, and, though Wilcox was defiant, potential investors were scared away.

Now came the first of Lean and Spiegel's many major trials. Marlon Brando dropped out of the production, preferring instead to take the role of Fletcher Christian in *Mutiny on the Bounty*. (Lean would later spend several years attempting to remake the story of Bligh and Christian in an ambitious two-part production, scripted by Robert Bolt.) They now had permission to film TE's story, but no one to play him.

Finney

The next choice was Albert Finney, then twenty-four and appearing in the West End in *Billy Liar*. In August 1960, Lean spent four days – and, according to rumour, a very great deal of money (£100,000[56]) shooting screen tests. Spiegel thought that, despite his northern

proletarian background, Finney would make a convincing Lawrence. Lean was less sure, and was willing only to tell Spiegel that he thought he could 'drag' Finney through the part. No dragging was necessary: Finney, declaring himself unwilling to become a 'movie star', turned them down.

The need for a plausible Lawrence was growing urgent. There was speculation that the part would go to Guinness; but at forty-six, Guinness was now too old to be a plausible Lawrence of Arabia on film. Lean began to haunt cinemas. 'One day I went to a film called *The Day They Robbed the Bank of England* ... And there was Peter O'Toole, playing a sort of silly-ass

Albert Finney

Englishman in a trout fishing scene. I said, "I'm going to use him as Lawrence."' In fact, O'Toole had already been strongly recommended by Lean's close friend Audrey Hepburn.

Spiegel dissented: 'I tell you, he's no good. I know it.' Spiegel's path had crossed O'Toole's when he was making *Suddenly Last Summer* (1959), and was scouting for a replacement for Montgomery Clift. The incorrigibly waggish O'Toole improvised the role of a brain surgeon for his test. He concluded by looking directly into the camera and saying, 'It's all right, Mrs Spiegel, but your son will never play violin again.' O'Toole tested for Lawrence on 7 November 1960. Two days later he was offered the part, for a fee of £12,500. He was required to make himself free from 1 December 1960, giving him four months in which to learn how to ride a camel.

Other casting

Sherif Ali ibn el Kharish. The first choice was Horst Bucholz, a twenty-eight-year-old German actor known to cinema audiences as one of *The Magnificent Seven* (1950), but he was already under contract to Billy Wilder. The next was the twenty-five-year-old Alain Delon – not yet a famous actor. He was signed, and Lean went straight to Jordan for an initial recce. Soon, though, Delon also dropped out. Spiegel ordered the Paris office of Columbia to provide dossiers of any young actor who might be suitable for the part, and eventually picked Maurice Ronet. He was signed to the production on 11 April 1961.

The major British and other non-Arab roles were less of a problem to cast:

General Allenby: Jack Hawkins, for £25,000. (Cary Grant and
    Laurence Olivier had also been considered.)
Colonel Brighton: Anthony Quayle. (£10,000).
General Murray: Donald Wolfit.
Mr Dryden: Claude Rains.

The Bey: Jose Ferrer. ($25,000, plus a brand-new $5,000 Porsche, for a week's work.)

The 'Arabs':
Alec Guinness: Feisal.
Anthony Quinn: Auda Abu Tayi.

Lean wanted Kirk Douglas for the role of the American reporter, but Douglas asked for too high a fee and above-the-title billing. The part went to Edmund O'Brien.

Wilson encore

On 4 August 1960, Wilson delivered his first draft screenplay. Lean read it carefully, and his notes to Wilson are impressively clear-sighted.

Prologue is too long and at the moment not related to theme ... Lose the Desert Song quality wherever it exists ... Do we want to make a western? Must not fall into visual cliché ... Too many train raids, which do not contribute to L's character. We lose the theme, the drive to unite the tribes. Many faceted aspects of Lawrence's character not yet in the screenplay. Example: masochism. Other examples: vanity vs shyness, solitude vs gregariousness, glimpses of his pride in the British ... Let us not avoid or censor out the homosexual aspect of Lawrence's relationships. The incipient homosexuality of Daud and Farraj must be emphasised.[57]

On 14 November 1960, Lean returned to Jordan to finish scouting locations. About four weeks later, Wilson flew out to see him with his second draft. Lean told him, bluntly, that it still did not satisfy him. Wilson was furious. He delivered one last draft, on 31 January 1961, and collected the last instalment of his $100,000 fee. (He insisted that his resignation should have no effect on his right to a screen credit. Spiegel proposed that he could have a screen credit if he signed a statement denying any connection with the Communist

Party. Wilson refused.) The production which had been in need of a star was now in urgent need of a writer. Spiegel chose three:

1. David Garnett, the seventy-year-old son of TE's publisher friend Edward Garnett. He signed a contract for £2,500 on 26 January 1961: his job was essentially that of tinkering with Wilson's script.
2. Beverly Cross, a young playwright who was soon to have a West End hit with the fluffy comedy *Boeing-Boeing*, had signed on the day before Garnett as 'Continuity Writer' for £3,000, and at once flew out to Jordan. Cross enjoyed his assignment, but admitted that his main contribution was to play nanny to O'Toole when he went off to the fleshpots of Beirut.
3. And Robert Bolt.

Enter Bolt

Robert Bolt's play *A Man for All Seasons* had opened in London on 1 July 1960. It ran for 320 performances, and propelled Bolt from relative obscurity to the front rank of British playwrights. It also caught the attention of Baroness Moura Budberg – a former mistress of Maxim Gorky, and a close friend of Sam Spiegel. Bolt's writing, she thought, had all the qualities Spiegel needed for his rewrite. Bolt knew how to shape complicated historical matter into forms that were dramatically appealing and yet reasonably faithful to the record; he could render abstract political and philosophical issues in urgent, concrete terms; his dialogue was trenchant and witty.

Bolt was born in Manchester in 1924, the son of a Methodist who ran a furniture shop. (Bolt's background had a good deal in common with Lean's: a puritanical family, a brother who was considered 'more brilliant', a wasted year or so in office work ...). He attended Manchester Grammar and read English at Manchester University, though his studies were interrupted by war service in the RAF. He also joined the Communist Party for a brief period. After

Robert Bolt on
location

graduation, he went on to be an English teacher. He had become a
full-time writer in 1958.

Bolt's reaction to Spiegel's approach was cool. 'I was a
playwright, not a scriptwriter, so I was insulted. What, a film?! …'
But he went to see Spiegel anyw¶ay.

He talked and talked, and offered me a cigar, and whisky. I glanced at the
label. It read, 'Specially bottled in the Highland of Scotland for Sam Spiegel.' I
should have known then that one doesn't win with Sam Spiegel …[58]

The producer explained their plight. Lean was stuck out in
Jordan, technically ready to start shooting but lacking a script with
speakable dialogue. What they needed was a quick rewrite. 'I was
quite outraged,' Bolt recalled. 'I explained that I was a playwright

and didn't do things like that. Eventually he said he would pay me ... I forget how much – say £10,000 for seven weeks' work.'[59] Bolt's mind was changed, but only briefly. On the way back to his house in Richmond, he read the script and felt that it was in need of far more than a polish. When he reached home, he phoned Spiegel and turned down the assignment again; again, Spiegel used his powers of persuasion.

His contract was signed on 17 February 1961, and committed him to twenty weeks of work, backdated to 2 January 1961. For a fee of £15,000, to be paid in weekly instalments, he would be required to write 'a screenplay with reference to a script by Michael Wilson based upon the life and exploits of Lawrence of Arabia'.[60] With only a few weeks in hand, Bolt took just about the only course open to him: return to the text of *Seven Pillars*, treat it as if it were a flawlessly accurate history, cut ruthlessly, condense characters, simplify the narrative. Thus, the large cast of British officers who saw active service in the desert campaign are boiled down into the single character of Colonel Brighton; while the diplomats and Middle-Eastern experts are summed up in the deliciously sly Dryden.

As to his central character: Bolt's verdict on Lawrence's political identity was unusual. He believed that TE was 'a romantic fascist', akin to the Spanish Carlists who had supported the claims of Don Carlos to the Spanish throne when his brother, King Ferdinand VII, declared that his heir would be his daughter, Isabella. Oddly, he chose not to make Lawrence aware of the Sykes–Picot treaty (see earlier). His Lawrence became more flamboyant than Wilson's, and he followed a suggestion of Lean's by transplanting, so to speak, Lawrence's better conscience into the character of Sherif Ali.

Almost everyone who read the pages that Bolt was producing thought that his solutions were inspired and his dialogue first-rate. Cast and other personnel were already massing in Jordan, money was starting to flow in alarming quantities and Spiegel decided to break his promise to Lean that they would not start shooting without a complete script. To his alarm, Lean heard that Horizon was booking a crew for a start date of 28 February 1961. (In reality, filming did not begin until 15 May 1961.)

Young

January 1961: Freddie Young, *Lawrence*'s Director of Photography, arrived in Jordan. He went up to Lean, held out his hand and said, 'Don't teach your grandmother to suck eggs.' He was echoing their first encounter, many years earlier. The ice was broken, and from this point on the two men got on swimmingly: Lean so trusted Young's grasp of what was required that he hardly ever gave any explicit instructions. Young then flew to Hollywood to select cameras and equipment. Lean had told him about the 'mirage shot' and said that he hadn't the faintest idea of how it might be achieved. Young found an extra-long lens in the Panavision stores, and saw that he had the tool he needed.

David Lean and Freddie Young

Apart from a completed script, all the elements were in place. And there was a new component: the experience of life in the desert. Throughout the Jordan shoot, Lean lived in a motor caravan which was mounted on the back of a Mercedes truck.

… you don't know what it's like living out in the desert. It's something unbelievable, the loneliness of it, the majesty of it, the wonder of the sky at night, whether it's starlight or moonlight. Just wonderful … When you're in the desert, you look into infinity. It's no wonder that nearly all the great religions came out of the desert.[61]

Eddie Fowlie was living in a caravan some twelve miles away from Lean:

The first night in the desert I turned on my little Zenith short-wave radio to try to find some news. And just as an enormous sun came up over the horizon – and it made my hair stand on end – the music from *Kwai* came on. And I thought, 'Christ, if that's not a good omen …'[62]

4 Shoot Part One: Jordan

For years we lived anyhow with one another in the naked desert, under the indifferent heaven. By day the hot sun fermented us; and we were dizzied by the beating wind. At night we were stained by dew, and shamed into pettiness by the innumerable silences of stars. We were a self-centred army without parade or gesture, devoted to freedom, the second of man's creeds, a purpose so ravenous that it devoured all our strength, a hope so transcendent that our earlier ambitions faded in its glare.

TE, *Seven Pillars of Wisdom*

The cameras finally began to turn over on 15 May 1961, at about three in the afternoon, a time of day when the Jordanian shadows are beginning to lengthen and the light losing some of its blinding intensity. The first shot of the *Lawrence* production was to be the audience's first view of the desert – that breath-stopping panorama which follows on immediately from the equally celebrated 'sunrise'

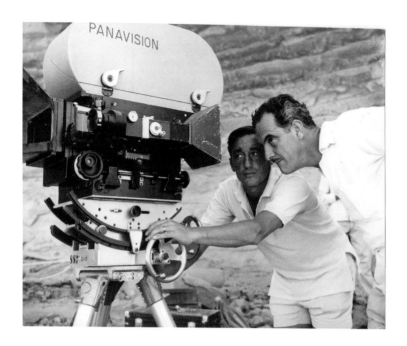

shot. (The sunrise was filmed by the second-unit cameraman, Peter Newbrook.) Lean's unit was on location at Jebel el Tubeiq, a mountain range roughly 250 miles to the east of Aqaba.

Every member of the 200-strong unit was wearing giant tinted goggles as protection against the glare and the sand and the 'khamsin' – the desert wind. The cameras – two 65mm Panavision models – were mounted on top of a 1,000-foot-high sand dune, after being dragged up an almost perpendicular slope on a sort of improvised ski-lift. Standing with these cameras were Lean, Freddie Young, the camera operator Ernest Day, and the first Assistant Director Roy Stevens. Lean – his face and arms now almost black after six months of scouting locations – began the shoot by waving his white hat at Stevens; but Stevens almost immediately called a halt. He had spotted a paper cup in camera range, and to send someone to remove it, and then brush away their footsteps, might easily mean an hour's delay.

Ernest Day and John Box

Eventually it blew away. The single greatest logistical problem on *Lawrence* would prove to be 'tidying' the desert between takes.

Lean called 'Action', and two camel riders – Lawrence and Tafas – came across the crest of the horizon. He had composed the shot so that it caught the effect of sand blowing from the top of the dune. The unit publicist, John Wollfenden, wrote that 'It creates an

Sweeping the desert

unearthly golden light as the grains whirl and eddy in fantastic patterns across the red sand carpet.'[63] The true journey of *Lawrence* had finally begun.

Crew

The basic crew for *Lawrence* was well over 200 strong; cast and extras could swell that figure beyond the 1,000 mark. As far as possible, Lean liked to work with people he already knew and trusted. Spiegel hired John Box, who had recently worked on *Our Man in Havana*, as the production designer. Two other key jobs were taken by women. Anne V. Coates, a relative newcomer who had cut the Finney screen test, was recruited as film editor, and Phyllis Dalton was made costume designer. The challenging job of production manager went to John Palmer; Phil Hobbs, who had worked wonders on *Kwai*, was appointed catering supervisor. Eddie Fowlie, who eventually became Lean's closest friend, was taken on as chief propman.

The production's main HQ, called Horizon 1, was set up in the former Indonesian Embassy on Jebel Webdeh in Amman. John Box and Phyllis Dalton operated from here. A young lady named Toni Gardiner ran the switchboard. King Hussein, who was always warmly supportive of the film as a sympathetic portrait of the Arab peoples and their cause, took a great shine to Miss Gardiner and, on 25 May 1961, Jordanian Independence Day, married her. She took the name of Mouna el Hussein: 'Desire of Hussein'. Anthony Nutting – a former high-ranking diplomat who had been hired as a technical adviser – complained that the telephones never worked properly after that.

Horizon 2 was established at Aqaba: Peter Dukelow, head of construction, oversaw the transformation of an old ex-army barracks into a habitable base with the help of Phil Hobbs. About a mile away from the barracks was the Beach Camp, which had a canteen, a formal dining hall and a bar – the Star Tavern Middle East Branch, decorated with posters for Guinness and Watney's.

All these preparations took place in the cooler months of the winter, to allow everyone to become slowly acclimatised. Horizon 3

King Hussein with
David Lean

was the designated name of any given location base – the canvas
towns inhabited by 'Lean's Mobile Maniacs'. In the last weeks
before shooting, Lean had been seething with frustration, but there
was still no definitive script. Spiegel had arrived in his yacht and
moored it off the Aqaba coast. John Box recalls that Spiegel was
untypically gloomy at this point, and talked of closing the
production down. Lean took a hard line: on *Kwai* he had banked
$1 million, and Spiegel $3 million. From *Lawrence* Lean could
expect $3 million and Spiegel about $9 million. So could they please
get on with it? Things began to look up when Bolt came to work on
the script with Lean. Bolt remembered discussing the passage in
which Lawrence speaks to Allenby about the execution of Gasim.
Lawrence is ...

... saying how guilty he feels, and then mentions that there's 'something else,'
apart from the guilt.

David said, 'What is something else, Robert?'

I said, 'Well, he sort of enjoyed it.'

David's script went up in the air. 'For heaven's sake, why don't you put it in.'[64]

. . . .

Astonishing as it now seems, there were no facilities for projecting rushes.[65] No one, not even Lean, was able to see what they had shot until they returned to London four months later. There was one early scare when reports came back from London that the negative had been marred with fingerprints; they demanded that all the camera crews be fingerprinted so that the culprit could be identified, even though it would have been all but impossible for them to touch the exposed film on site. Investigations soon revealed that the real culprit was someone in the labs.

Lean's policy for the first half of the film was, as far as possible, to shoot in continuity, so that O'Toole's performance would be shaped by much the same process of discovery that the audience would experience. He spent almost a month with just three actors – O'Toole, Maurice Ronet as Sherif Ali and Zia Mohyeddin as Tafas – filming the scenes of Lawrence and Tafas making their trek across the desert. Moyheddin, an Indian national, was new to films. He had made his name playing Dr Aziz in a London stage production of *A Passage to India*, and was quite unprepared for Lean's perfectionism.

His first scene was the pause in their long ride where he tells Lawrence 'Here you may drink. One cup.' It was a harsh baptism.

We began shooting at two-thirty and went on to six – we did twenty-five or thirty takes. Then David said, 'All right, we'll do it tomorrow.' I thought, Jesus, a big two-camera scene. The world's greatest director. What did I do wrong? There was no come back. He wasn't saying, too much or too little, none of the direction that one might expect. Weeks later he winked at me, and said he didn't want me to think it was going to be easy. It was a kind of sadism.[66]

In the evenings the three actors would go over the script with Lean, but it soon became clear to everyone that Lean was increasingly dissatisfied with Ronet. Moyheddin recalls that Lean was tempted to hand the role over to him, but the director ordered an index of Egyptian actors which he scoured until he came across the face of Omar Sharif. Since Ali grows into Lawrence's 'Better Half' – his brother, his (implicit) lover, his walking conscience – Lean needed a performer whose flagrant male beauty would not simply rival O'Toole's, but mirror it. At an unconscious level, the audience would be made to sense that Ali is the dark-skinned desert god to Lawrence's pale-skinned sun god.

Sharif

Sharif – real name Michael Shaloub – had been born into a wealthy Lebanese Christian family in 1932; his parents were friends with the royal family, later to be overthrown by President Nasser. He had made his film début young, in 1953, changing his name first to Omar Cheriff,

David Lean directing Omar Sharif

then to Sharif. He converted to Islam so as to be allowed to marry Faten Hamama, at that time the most famous actress in the Middle East. When Spiegel first approached him, he would have had almost every reason to refuse: all that was being offered was a screen test, for a small part, not yet written, and in a foreign country at that. But the name of David Lean was too tempting to resist; and Spiegel – for all that he was not merely Jewish but a known Zionist – somehow obtained an exit visa for him with no apparent difficulty. They flew to Tubeiq.

'We landed,' Sharif recalled, 'and there was one man standing in the desert and the plane taxied over to him. That was David Lean. He looked me over very sharply and took me to the make-up tent. He tried a beard and moustache on me, rejected the beard and then put me into a black costume. Then I was introduced to Peter O'Toole. Peter said no one is called Omar Sharif. Your name must be Fred. So he called me Cairo Fred.'[67]

It was the beginning of a close friendship between the two actors which helped lend subliminal depths of authenticity to their scenes together. Since Lean's skills as a director did not run to reassuring his cast, O'Toole and Sharif also came to rely on each other to keep their morale from sagging. At one point, O'Toole reached such a state of anxious despair that he seriously considered quitting, believing himself incompetent. He was helped back to confidence by a brief visit from his wife, Sian Phillips.

Sharif still had no idea which part he was lined up for when he flew back to Cairo, and then on to Columbia's London offices. He was paid just £8,000, told that he had landed the plum role of Ali, and was ordered to a plastic surgeon to have a mole removed from his face. He arrived back in Jordan to play Ali on 3 June 1961. He was given barely more than a week in which to learn how to ride a camel for his big entrance: probably the film's most memorable scene.

The great mirage entrance was filmed on 12 and 13 June 1961 on the salt flats of Al Jafr, thirty miles to the east of Ma'an. The crew hated it; to echo Dryden, in Bolt's script, the place was 'a burning, fiery furnace'. Howard Kent wrote that 'By comparison with Al Jafr, Tubeiq was paradise. If there is a divine purpose in Jafr it is that God has placed it on earth as a warning of what hell is like.'[68]

Lean used three cameras: Freddie Young, Ernest Day and Peter Newbrook were the operators. Eddie Fowlie and his team had dug a deep hole in the ground for the upwards shot from inside the well. John Box, who felt that there was something bland about the panorama, sent a painter to draw a white line in the sand towards the horizon from which Ali would appear. Then a row of black pebbles was laid next to it to accentuate the line. Young didn't like it, but Lean backed up Box's decision. Lean envisaged the scene as a single shot, so no doubles were used. He simply sent Sharif off on his camel – by a roundabout route, so that no camel tracks would appear in shot – and signalled him to ride back.

Freddie Young:

I used the long lens I found in Hollywood. We had Omar Sharif go practically out of sight until he was a little pinpoint in the distance and David told him to ride straight towards the camera. Nobody had done it before and nobody had done it in colour in 70mm.[69]

Peter Newbrook recalled that the whole take lasted almost ten minutes, beginning with nothing visible in his viewfinder and ending in a head-and-shoulders close-up. Lean took John Box aside and enthused: 'You'll never do a better bit of designing in films, ever!' The edited version of that footage is among the touchstones of world cinema, though Lean was never entirely contented with it. 'Originally I had Omar coming out of the mirage at double the length and it was better. I lost my nerve and cut quite a bit. Wish I hadn't.'[70]

The crew remained on location at Al Jafr for the next big scene – the sequence in which Lawrence rides back to rescue Gasim. Ali, in his first on-screen show of intense emotion, has to explode in rage.

It was a scene that was always scheduled to be done after lunch. But we never got to do it because of the sandstorms. Then one day we came to do it and my camel, a wonderful animal called Alia, was behaving badly and couldn't hit the mark. I was yelling and screaming and the camel was going nuts. That took a lot out of me and I started sobbing and had a sort of nervous breakdown.[71]

. . . .

Despite the best efforts of Phil Hobbs and others to provide them with some semblance of home comforts, the rank-and-file crew members grew discontented and decided to stage a revolt. Their main complaints were the obvious ones: sand, flies, cold showers, primitive latrines and temperatures that were already reaching as high as 118 degrees in the shade. (In summer, the temperatures could exceed 140 degrees.) The production manager, John Palmer, received an official complaint on 23 May 1961. These complaints dragged on for months, and in the end, after twenty-one weeks in the desert, the men duly received their claim for additional hardship money: two guineas a day.

Unmentioned by the men, but an additional cause for complaint, was the sheer boredom of life after work. 'It was like being in the army,' said Sharif. 'We sat in the bar and got pissed every night. There was nothing else to do.'[72] Whenever they could, O'Toole and Sharif jumped on the plane and went on three-day binges in Beirut. Everyone developed their own ways of coping. Lean would leave everyone else and go off to have dinner with his new mistress Barbara Cole, while listening to his beloved records of Stéphane Grappelli and Errol Garner. Guinness liked to swim in the Gulf of Aqaba, and to talk about Shakespeare. Sharif recalled him as an intensely private man who only became animated when he spoke about acting: 'He was an astonishing individual.'

. . . .

31 May 1961, Tubeiq: The crew filmed the 'miracle' scene in which Lawrence spends the night brooding, alone in the desert, and dreams up his plan for the attack on Aqaba. His two boy servants, watching him in bafflement, roll a stone gently down towards him. Lawrence appears not to react, but then slowly reaches behind his back, picks up the stone and clenches it in his fist. O'Toole: 'On paper it's just a bloke having a think. But the mixture of introspection and dynamism, what's implied by holding that stone, as if it were Aqaba itself, expressed a great deal, visually and emotionally.' In Bolt's script, Lawrence was meant to grip the stone so fiercely that his hand bleeds. At the last minute, Lean decided that this was over the top. Throughout the production, he was trying to balance artistic restraint against emotional power, and he suspected that he usually erred on the side of restraint. As he remarked

'A bloke having a think'

in a letter to Bolt: 'It's something to do with this English politeness I'm always talking about. We both want to say it … but don't *quite* want to say it. Too obvious. Too vulgar …'[73]

Wadi Rumm and Anthony Quinn

With shooting at Jebel Tubeiq and Al Jafr now completed, the crew moved to Wadi Rumm, a valley about twenty miles to the north-east of Aqaba. It is a magnificent setting, and, as Brownlow rightly notes, Lean used it much as John Ford used Monument Valley. An airstrip was built for the DC3s and the Dove: the Dove was used both to ferry cast and crew to Beirut every few weeks for much-needed R and R, and also to fly in major actors from England: Guinness, Quinn, Quayle.

Because the midday sun was too intense to permit any strenuous activity, the timetable for the filming day was divided into two halves. The first shoot would last from about eight till eleven, though Lean would sometimes linger over his breakfast and declare himself incapable of deciding what to do. When this happened, his usual resort was to listen again to the tapes of Robert Bolt acting out and discussing the scene they were about to film. After pondering the whole tape, he would usually leap into action as if there had never been any doubts in his mind.

Anthony Quinn arrived on the set in late August 1961. 'I had not met Lean until I got to Jordan. I arrived in the afternoon and they

Anthony Quinn as Auda

wanted me to see him immediately. I said I didn't want David to see me without my make-up on.' Charlie Parker, the make-up man, obliged, and Phyllis Dalton gave him a robe. Thus transformed, he went on to Wadi Rumm:

There were some five hundred Arabs sitting under the cliffs in the shade. They all got up and said Auda! Auda! They all followed me. We walked through the sand and saw David rehearsing the scene with Peter and the dagger. I didn't move but the Arabs behind me kept shouting Auda! Auda! Auda Abu Tayi! Then David turned around and said 'Good God, who's that? Cancel Quinn and get that man to play Auda.'[74]

The scene for which Quinn had arrived was an untypical piece of improvisation by O'Toole – Lean did not usually approve of improvisation. The director had said to O'Toole: 'There's something missing here. What do you think a young man would do alone in the desert if he's just been handed these beautiful robes? There's your theatre. Do what you like.' O'Toole thought that Lawrence would want to look at himself. 'There's no water or mirrors in the desert so I had the idea of pulling out my knife and looking in the blade. I can still hear David behind the camera saying "Clever boy!" ...'[75] Mad magazine, in a telling parody of the film, rendered this scene with a cartoon of Lawrence singing Maria's song 'I Feel Pretty' from West Side Story (1957): one of many contemporary references to the unexpectedly feminine qualities of the screen Lawrence.

Bolt in prison

Back in the UK, Robert Bolt had taken part in a mass demonstration organised by the Campaign for Nuclear Disarmament. Some 10,000 people gathered in Trafalgar Square and Whitehall, and Bolt was among those arrested. 12 September 1961: in the company of Lord and Lady Russell, the playwright Arnold Wesker and other members of the Committee of 100, Bolt attended Bow Street Magistrate's Court. Since they all refused to be bound over to keep the peace, they

were all sentenced to short terms of imprisonment: Lord and Lady
Russell for a week, Bolt and the rest to a month. As many pointed
out, the author of *A Man for All Seasons* could hardly be expected to
recant. Bolt spent two days in Brixton before being transferred to
Drake Hall Open Prison in Staffordshire. His cellmate was the poet
Christopher Logue (who went on, in the footsteps of Lawrence, to be
a famous translator of Homer: see *War Music*.) The regime was soft,
but there was one significant point of discipline: to write for money
was forbidden. Anything he wrote while in gaol automatically
became government property, and could be confiscated. As long as
Bolt remained in prison, the script could not be completed.

Shutdown

On 28 September 1961, the 117th day of production, the film was
shut down. Accounts of why this was the case differ. One was very
simple: Bolt had barely begun to work on the film's second half, and
Lean would soon have nothing left to film. Spiegel drove out to
Drake Hall:

Bolt: 'And then all hell broke loose. Sam Spiegel just went absolutely mad –
"So have these people got to lose their jobs and lose thousands of dollars just
so that you can go to heaven when you die?" was his line. So after a fortnight
I bound myself over and came out. I felt that although there were very good
reasons why I should, I knew that ultimately I should *not* have come out, and
it was simply because Sam had built up the pressure to such an extent that I
couldn't hold out.'[76]

It swiftly dawned on Bolt that he had, to put it bluntly, been
conned. He could have served out his remaining two weeks and it
would have made no difference, since the production had shut down
anyway. Lean and Spiegel knew that they would not commence
shooting until Christmas, and had budgeted accordingly. Bolt said
that it was 'the most shameful moment of my life.'[77] Many
commentators have noted the parallels between Bolt's sense of having

sold out and Lawrence's sense, in the film's second half, of having been an unwitting traitor to the Arab cause.

Other versions of the shutdown have Lean as the injured party.

Money

Less than a month into shooting, Columbia had already begun to be alarmed about the mounting costs of the production. Leo Jaffe, the Head of Columbia in New York, was told by Bill Graf that *Lawrence* might take as much as $10 million to complete: Spiegel had assured them it would not cost more than $3 million. Distrusting Spiegel's estimates, Jaffe proposed that 'a strong position be taken now to terminate Jordan shooting not later than 11 September as scheduled and then try to finalise pic at the $8 million maximum mark.'[78] His colleagues agreed, and determined that the costly Jordan location be abandoned as soon as possible; the rest of the film could be shot in Spain.

Spiegel also agreed. He was now convinced that Lean had become another 'desert-loving Englishman', obsessed with staying out in the wilderness as long as possible. He began arrangements for the Wadi Rumm camp to be dismantled and the equipment shipped to Spain. John Box recalls that when he passed on news of Spiegel's decision by letter '[Lean] had to be dragged screaming from his caravan.'[79] Lean wrote Spiegel a passionate letter from Wadi Rumm, which 'is being pulled down this very minute.' It may have served no greater practical purpose than to vent his rage;[80] but it was one of his most eloquent statements of what he was trying to achieve:

The thing that's going to make this a very exceptional picture in the world-beater class are the backgrounds, the camels, horses, and *uniqueness* of the strange atmosphere we are putting around our intimate story. Audiences have seen good scenes and good characters before; they haven't seen what we are showing them to date in the first half of this picture. This is our great spectacle which will pull the crowd from university professor to newsboy. For God's sake, I beg of you, don't underestimate it. This can be one of the greats. It's the most wonderful combination of spectacle and intimate character study which ever fell into a filmmaker's lap. Don't muff it. I don't say this to you because of some so-called creative fad. I know where I'm going and I know my job.[81]

John Box quietly agreed with Spiegel that the move to Spain was wise: 'There was no way we could have built Cairo or Damascus out there ... The unit was exhausted, we were losing people, they had to be flown home and medicine and replacements flown out.' But he shared Lean's grief:

I tell you what, I cried. I didn't want to leave the desert. I really did give the family terrible trouble when I came back because I couldn't adjust to anything. The desert was pure. But we had to leave.[82]

The company dispersed for eleven weeks.

5 Shoot Part Two: Spain, Morocco, England

For fear of being hurt, or rather to earn five minutes' respite from a pain which drove me mad, I gave away the only possession we are born into the world with – our bodily integrity. It's an unforgivable matter, an irrecoverable position: and it's that which has made me forswear decent living, and the exercise of my not-contemptible wits and talents. You may call this morbid: but think of the offence, and the intensity of my brooding over it for these years. Consider wandering around the decent ghosts hereafter, crying 'Unclean unclean!'.

TE to Mrs Charlotte Shaw, 26 March 1924[83]

Seville

Three weeks after his release from prison, Bolt flew to Spain. He wrote a glum letter to his father: 'I finish work on the script of *Lawrence* on December 18th, whether it's finished or not. I've had all I can take of that set-up.'[84] In the event, he was to stay on with Lean for a full three months, and actually made a brief, silent appearance

Robert Bolt (centre) with pipe

in the film as a British officer, glimpsed puffing on a pipe as Lawrence sways Allenby towards supporting the Arab Revolt.

Gloomy or not, he was writing brilliantly, and finding new ways of making the intricate latter parts of *Seven Pillars* not only comprehensible but charged with drama and bitter ironies. Lean was, in Adrian Turner's words,

thrilled by [Bolt's] grasp of narrative and his way with dialogue. Whereas Wilson's screenplay was an often turgid account of tribal politics and imperial imperatives, [Bolt] stripped the story to its essentials, dispensed with speeches and arrived at a tone which frequently borders on satire.

Bolt also found a way of moulding his source material so that it should play to one of his strengths as a dramatist: the interplay of two starkly contrasting characters – Lawrence the wayward, driven 'son', Allenby the rock-solid 'father'.

Shooting resumed in Seville on 18 December 1961. In most respects, life was a lot easier: both cast and crew were now based in good hotels, some of which did double duty as locations. The Alfonso XIII, built in the 1920s, stood in for the Officers' Club in Cairo. The Plaza de Espana, built in 1929, became Allenby's HQ. At the same time, John Box dressed up a former casino as the Damascus Town Hall, and made other Damascene buildings from structures on the Plaza of the Americas.

Lawrence as Sun God

In an early encounter between Lawrence and Dryden, the diplomat tries to chasten his headstrong protégé: 'Only two kinds of creature get fun in the desert – Bedouins and Gods; and you're neither.' Lawrence disagrees; and so, in their way, did Bolt and Lean. As the director told Bolt:

I had gods with suns [i.e. statues and carvings of solar deities] behind them [Rains and O'Toole] and got Claude Rains to speak the lines with warning and

significance. Having got so far I got frightened and shot the scene in un-committing medium shot, kidding myself it would be best to have no close-ups because they would take away from the impact of the match-blowing close-up at the end … I *should* have gone much further. I should have arranged Peter in such a position that he had a bloody great sun-god plaque right behind his close-up, so that when he stood on top of the train, the sun behind him, the audience would subconsciously connect it with the 'warning' in the office …

Enter – and Exit – O'Brien

Edmund O'Brien was cast to play the role of Jackson Bentley, the film's equivalent of Lowell Thomas. (The name was changed, and the part significantly diminished, when Bolt took over Wilson's screenplay.) He arrived in Seville in January, and seems to have stayed long enough to shoot two or three scenes. O'Brien then flew home for a break in Los Angeles, where he almost immediately had a heart attack. It would have been too expensive to wait for his recovery, so Lean recruited Arthur Kennedy. O'Brien's few scenes were re-shot with Kennedy, but O'Brien can still be glimpsed in the finished film, walking from the background into the foreground as Lawrence and the club secretary chat about squash courts.

Claude Rains as Dryden; note sun image in background

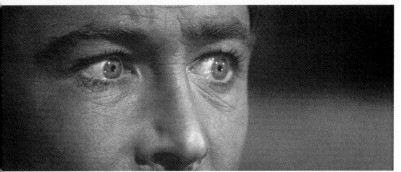

Deraa

12 March 1962. Jose Ferrer arrived to play his role as the Turkish Bey, for the crucial scene at the Deraa barracks in which Lawrence, having fallen into the hands of the enemy, is tortured and – to all but the most innocent eyes – raped. A Puerto Rican, Ferrer spoke impeccable Spanish, and made a striking, imperious figure on set. But Lean was not satisfied. He wrote to Bolt:

At the end of the Bey scene we should have had just one more beat to explain that he had been defiled by the Bey – which was missed by ninety percent of our audiences.[85] Our failures within a particular film spring, I think, from our not taking enough care and falling back on an attitude of, well, if they don't get it ... and bugger them. [sic][86]

Jose Ferrer as the Bey

Lawrence as ghost

Lean:

One of the cleverest things in *Lawrence*, I'm not sure whose idea it was –
probably John Box's – concerned the Arab robes. Lawrence is given these
robes fairly early on, when he's accepted by the Arabs, and then the rot starts
to set in, and he is seized by a sort of power mania. What the costume people
did was gradually to change the texture of the material from which his Arab
cloths were made, and they made it thinner and thinner until it was just
muslin, and at the end he looked almost ghostlike.[87]

Bolt:

The end of the film was shot so you never see Lawrence's face. When Feisal
has his parting line, we cut and all we see are these diaphanous curtains and
the shadow of Lawrence behind them … And when he is in the car we got a
very tall driver and sat him on some cushions so his face was clearly visible.
Lawrence's face was behind the dusty windscreen so we could hardly see
him. He was like a ghost.[88]

Almeria

19 March 1962: the unit moved on from Seville to Almeria on the
Mediterranean coast. The location was discovered by Andre De Toth,
who had been despatched with John Box by Lean. De Toth, a polyglot
Hungarian director, was a macho, larger-than-life piratical character.
True to his swashbuckling reputation, De Toth flew his own small
plane across the country, in search of plausibly Arabian landscapes. He
then joined the production full time as one of the second unit directors.

At the time, Almeria was an impoverished fishing village;
Lawrence transformed it for ever. Lean bought some land there, with
a view to building a holiday home, as did John Box, Eddie Fowlie
and Barbara Cole. Soon, it would become famous as the key location
for spaghetti Westerns. It was a harsh, barren territory, and really
nothing very much like the sublime desertscapes of Jordan, but Lean
and Box had ways of tackling that problem. Most of the action
sequences would be filmed at close quarters, so that the audience

would hardly be aware of the change in scenery; and the scenery itself could be modified. The drab sand, for example, was not to Lean's taste, so Fowlie imported quantities of yellow sand to dress it up.

Among the scenes to be filmed here were the storming of Aqaba, and Lawrence's attacks on the Hejaz railways. The Aqaba set was built on a beach called Playa del Algorocibo, near Carboneros. It was made up of some 300 separate structures – most of them no more than bare façades, designed to be photographed only from the landward side – built mainly from stones dug out of a dried-up river bed. This excavation work also served the purpose of giving a clearer run for the cavalry charge. While Aqaba was under construction, the second unit started work on the train-wrecking scenes. A steam locomotive had been transported by road to the location, a place called Cabo del Gato, where the production team had laid a mile of track.

Lean arrived in time to take over direction for the scene in which Lawrence is shot by a wounded Turkish soldier, and for Lawrence's triumphal walk along the roof of the train. Pursuing the 'solar deity' metaphor, he defied conventional wisdom and shot O'Toole with the sun blazing behind him. O'Toole should have been reduced to nothing more than a featureless silhouette, but the shot is exhilarating. As a young camera buff, Lean had proved to himself that it was often possible to take 'impossible' shots, and the lesson never left him.

Arthur Kennedy as Jackson Bentley – the character based on Lowell Thomas

De Toth left the production soon after this sequence was in the can. Nicolas Roeg reflected that 'The second-unit director really wants to make his own film. He sees things and has ideas that really cannot fit. Our second unit got a bit out of hand …'[89] To Roeg's surprise, Lean made him second-unit director in De Toth's place.

Aqaba

Lean planned to film the set from just one angle, though he knew that this might be a risky stratagem. His certainty about the idea is vindicated by the outcome on screen, as magnificent as it is elegant. The camera looks down from a great height on the Arab cavalry pouring in from the desert, then pans across the (fake) town and ends with the fixed – and thus useless – Turkish gun pointing out to sea. John Box:

It was a very bold shot. Several times I said to [Lean] 'Aren't we going over the top? What about a cut?' 'No John,' he said, 'Be bold.' He had the ability to do it. I think that sequence shows what good movie-making is all about.[90]

The very first shot of the film, the overhead of Lawrence, was filmed in Almeria on 24 June 1962. Lawrence's Brough had been shipped to Spain, and was mounted on a wooden platform painted to look like paving stones.

Morocco

It had soon become obvious to everyone that Spain could not provide enough suitable locations: above all, there was no stretch of desert large and bleak enough to provide a backdrop for the massacre sequence. Eyes turned towards North Africa. Deals were made. 10 May 1962: Norman Spencer set up a production office in Casablanca. He spent the better part of the next two months in a wearying round of negotiations with government ministers, the Moroccan Army and assorted entrepreneurs. At every turn there seemed to be a fresh problem: there were not enough camels; the local troops demanded pay increases; the water supply proved to be contaminated with salt.

June 1962: Lean drove Barbara Cole and Freddie Young in his Rolls Royce from Almeria to Gibraltar, where the car was ferried across to Morocco. After a brief meeting with Spencer, they drove on to Marrakesh. The main location was to be Ouarzazate, about nine hours' drive from Casablanca into the desert. It had been chosen for its ugliness. Quinn called it 'the asshole of the world'. Their production facilities were shipped from Spain by freighter, then loaded onto thirty 'Queen Marys' – the giant trucks that the RAF had used in World War II to transport planes by road. Most of the crew flew in to the location; and they saw how tough conditions were going to be. 'Everyone went off their heads,' said Spencer. 'The heat, the conditions, the wind, the living in tents …' Illnesses, from rashes to enteritis to malaria, plagued the set. The Moroccan troops, meanwhile, were in a state of disaffection verging on revolt. The wages they were supposed to have been paid vanished into a bank account in Paris, and before long, the troops reached such a nadir of morale that they started firing live shots over the heads of Lean and his team.[91]

A production progress report logged on 21 July 1962 – the day set for filming the Arab army as it assembles for the push on Damascus – showed that Lean had thus far averaged a total of twenty-four seconds of footage per day: barely one-sixth of the usual

rate for Hollywood productions at that time. When it came time to start shooting the bloodbath, the terrible state of morale was all too obvious. Norman Spencer remembers that 'On the first charge, some of the camels collapsed and died ... And then we found that some of the Moroccans were deliberately injuring their camels so that they could claim damages against us. ...'[92]

Despite it all, Lean managed the scene triumphantly, conveying the due horror of Tafas without wallowing excessively in blood and guts. The key shot – a grim echo of Lawrence's narcissistic gaze into his dagger – showed Lawrence staring in terror and disbelief at his own image reflected in his blood-drenched knife. The Sun God has

Before and after

become Kurtz. Kevin Brownlow (1996) notes how rare it was for Hollywood film-makers to portray a super-hero committing a crime against humanity; without this integrity on the part of Bolt and Lean, the film would be a far slighter work.

Towards the end of the Moroccan shoot, Spiegel flew in to give everyone a pep talk. The burden of his remarks was that he was proud of everybody, and didn't mind at all that the film would probably fail to turn a profit … but please, please, go faster! Since Lean was the only one who had the authority to set the pace of production, Spiegel took him aside for a personal lament. Lean gave in. On 18 August he went back to England, leaving Roeg and his second unit to film some close-ups for the massacre.

Filming the memorial service scene

England

Lean's first business in England was to have an operation on his eye.
Since he had often disdained to wear protective goggles in the desert –
he claimed that they interrupted his chain of thought – he was
suffering from the effects of sand embedded behind his eyelid. The
rest of the shoot went swiftly, though not without incident. On 8
September 1962, Lean shot the memorial service sequence at St
Paul's. On 14 September, he went to Chobham, Surrey, to film the
motorbike sequence. (A note for pedants: Box and Fowlie gave the
bike the registration number UL656; but UL656 was the machine TE
had owned fom 1929 to 1932. The bike on which he crashed was
GW2275.)

Having gone through sixteen months of filming with nothing
much worse than boils, sores, bruises and hangovers, O'Toole now
had his most dangerous moment, when a safety chain on his
motorcycle broke. He narrowly escaped serious injury. The very last
shot to be filmed was of Lawrence's goggles hanging from a branch.
Bolt's script proposed that the goggles should come sliding down the
road towards the camera, but on camera the effect proved
unappealing. The date was 21 September 1962. Sum total of days of
shooting: 313. The production had lasted almost as long as the Arab
Revolt itself.

Post-production

Lean moved into the flat above the Warwick Films cutting rooms in South Audley Street. Anne Coates already had two hours' worth of rough-cut material and nine hours of rushes, including the Moroccan footage. They launched into a punishing regime: 9.00 am to midnight, seven days a week. Lean, who could be so stern when directing, became a different person entirely in the cutting room: light-hearted, funny, generous.

They cut the second half of the film first, because it had complex sound requirements – the train wrecking, the massacre – and the technicians needed as much time as could be squeezed. As Lean admitted, the Sound Department, under Winston Ryder, worked virtual miracles in the time allotted to them:

I'm terribly conscious of the sound track, which is almost as important as the pictures. For example, when Omar Sharif comes out of the desert, Win Ryder put in the pad, pad, pad of the camel's feet. It wasn't a real sound, but it added immeasurably to the silence of the desert, the size of it all.[93]

So many technicians were called in to work on the film that they overflowed the cutting rooms at Shepperton and had to be housed in caravans. Minor disaster followed minor disaster: the sand, needed for post-synching of most of the desert scenes, was dumped outside in pouring rain, and would have sounded more like thick mud. After a few weeks, Lean and Coates sent off a completed version of the second half, expecting to have a chance to refine it later; in the event, there simply was not time for any more editing. Just as Lean was arriving back in England, Spiegel had negotiated for *Lawrence* to be shown at a Royal Film Performance on 10 December 1962: less than four months for the entire post-production, including one more brief shoot.

Filming resumed, for one day only, on Saturday, 6 October 1962. Lean was dissatisfied with a close-up in the mirage sequence – the one in which Lawrence declares, 'Sherif Ali, so long as the Arabs fight tribe against tribe …'. O'Toole recalled how strange the process was:

So having been in the wilderness of Zin, we find ourselves in the relative wilderness of Hammersmith in a tiny little room with an old blue wall and a bit of dry ice ... He showed me [the edited footage] and it was extraordinary, for I was 27 in the first shot; cut to the figure coming through the mirage; 29 in the second shot and 27 in the third. The difference was astounding. I'd lost the bloom of youth. We're in a strange situation, film actors. We can watch the process of decomposition in the flesh.[94]

Music

Maurice Jarre's score became such a powerful element in the film's triumph that it is hard to believe how late in the production he was recruited, and how little time he was allowed. Lean's original choice of composer had been Malcolm Arnold, who had written the music for *Kwai*. Spiegel had what seemed an even better idea: commission Sir William Walton to write the dramatic themes, and have Arnold orchestrate and conduct them. But the English composers spurned them.

Spiegel then had the idea to split the film's score into two, with an 'Eastern' set of themes to be provided by the Soviet composer Aram Khachaturian and the British themes by Benjamin Britten. He also sent for the young French composer Maurice Jarre, whose job would be to co-ordinate the two composers' work. Jarre came to London, was set up in Half Moon Street, and began to write his own themes. But Khachaturian could not gain permission to leave the USSR, and Britten demanded at least a year to complete the work.

Jarre was in the course of making a successful transition from composition for concert halls to writing for films. A former collaborator with Pierre Boulez, he had created scores for two major French directors, Alain Resnais and Georges Franju, and had recently finished work on another high-budget war film, *The Longest Day*. With Britten and Khachaturian out of the picture, he reasonably hoped that the assignment would be his alone. Spiegel, however, decided to turn to a well-known composer of a very different kind.

He flew to New York, and came back crowing that he had done a great deal with Richard Rodgers, of Rodgers and Hammerstein.

By the middle of September, Rodgers had produced a handful of themes – including, for some reason, a 'love theme' (Lawrence and Ali?). Spiegel called Lean and Jarre to a meeting at which a pianist played them the results. Lean was underwhelmed, especially when the pianist recognised one of the tunes as an old military march: 'Sam, what is all this rubbish?' Spiegel turned to Jarre and asked him if he had anything to show for his weeks under contract. Jarre went to the keyboard and picked out a yearning tune – the main theme. Lean was delighted, and told Spiegel that Jarre was precisely in tune with his film's ethos and should be given the job. Jarre was allowed just six weeks to have his complete score ready for recording – though the task was lightened a little by Lean's wish to include an existing military march, 'The Voice of the Guns', composed by Kenneth Alford, who also wrote the immortal 'Colonel Bogey'.

Always craving prestige, Spiegel had arranged for the London Philharmonic Orchestra to perform the compositions under the baton of Sir Adrian Boult, at Shepperton Studios. But Boult soon discovered that the art of conducting for movies required a degree of accuracy that was beyond him. He handed the baton gracefully over to Jarre; but his name remained on the credits.

. . . .

Paul Valery famously observed that works of art are never completed, only abandoned. As the deadline of the world première, 10 December, drew nearer, Lean found himself increasingly discontented with the pace of the film, especially in its second half. He wanted to fine-tune some sequences, and make some larger cuts. By the time he reluctantly handed the film over for its final 70mm grading, *Lawrence of Arabia* was running at 222 minutes. It was time for the world to see what he had made.

6 Release and Reactions: 1962

One of the sorest things in life is to come to realise that one is just not good enough. Better perhaps than some, than many, almost – but I do not care for relatives, for matching myself against my kind. There is an ideal standard somewhere and only that matters: and I cannot find it.

TE to Eric Kennington, 6 August 1934[95]

Monday, 10 December 1962 saw the world première of *Lawrence of Arabia* at the Odeon, Leicester Square. For the last week, southern England had been in the grip of freezing fog: 340 people had died, public transport was crippled. There was a last-minute panic in the Lean camp, too. Only two 70mm prints had been prepared, one for London, one for New York, and the London version proved to have a scratched reel. Anne Coates had to make her way over to Heathrow airport and seize the suitable can in time for the Sunday-morning technical run.

The last weeks had been so rushed that until that Sunday morning, no one had seen the completed film straight through. Even for the grading, they had watched the second half first; and they had been used to watching 35mm CinemaScope reductions and black-and-white dubbing dupes. Anne Coates went to the tech run and saw the real thing for the first time. Everyone was stunned; overpowered by its sheer, immoderate beauty.

The following night, some 2,000 guests, including Her Majesty Queen Elizabeth II, fought their way through the fog to a gala opening. The band of the Royal Horse Guards provided the fanfare, and the Welsh Guards band played the National Anthem. It was an incongruously military launch for a film which embodies views of military action which range from the disenchanted to the horrified. The night held some wounds for Lean's pride. 'Ah, good evening', said Prince Philip to Lean. 'Good flick?' 'I hope so, sir.' 'Now,' Lean reflected in later years, 'he had no intention of being insulting, or talking down. But we were "the flicks". And that is still the way the English Establishment feels about the movies …'[96]

Overall, though, Lean had no reason to feel disgruntled. The response was overwhelming; his film was unanimously proclaimed magnificent. The *Lawrence* team went on to a jubilant party at Grosvenor House. Spiegel confessed that what Lean had done vastly exceeded his expectations. TE's friend Noël Coward quipped that if O'Toole had looked any prettier they would have had to call the film 'Florence of Arabia'.

Lean feared and loathed critics, but in this case he had little to worry about. With one or two exceptions, British reviews ranged from the decidedly positive to the glowing. Mild dissidents included Penelope Gilliatt of *The Observer*, who found it: 'a thoughtful picture with an intensely serious central performance, but it doesn't hold together in great excitement.'[97] John Coleman of the *New Statesman* was far more dismissive, concluding that '… none of it is good enough. Setting to one side the obligatory, contemptible music, the film never decisively makes up its mind what it's after – a breathing portrait of Lawrence or a series of sandy battles and torments.'[98]

A more typical note was struck by Alexander Walker in the *Evening Standard*:

Here is an epic with intellect behind it. An unforgettable display of action staged with artistry. A momentous story told with moral force. What on earth has wrought this miracle? The makers.

Producer Sam Spiegel is a man of culture as well as finance. David Lean is a director who goes out to the wild place [sic] to meditate on his films, much as prophets used to contemplate unworldly things. Scriptwriter Robert Bolt is our subtlest playwright of men's emotions. And I think that Allah, in the shape of F. A. Young's Technicolor camerawork, poured down his blessing for the two years of filming. An unbeatable team![99]

The apotheosis was reached by Dilys Powell in the *Sunday Times*, 16 December 1962:

Romantic landscapes, august landscapes – one has seen these often enough on the screen. This is something else. The sun rising on the rim of blood-orange sand; dust storms like the smoke-trails of a djinn; the shapes of infinity, the colours of heat – I think it is the first time for the cinema to communicate ecstasy. *Lawrence of Arabia* is full of such beauties, and I can't refrain from singling out the ambush of a train-load of horses and the capture in particular of one proud milk-white creature – a passage which might be out of Homer …

Lawrence of Arabia taken as a whole is a genuine, sometimes even a profound interpretation of character. And that alone, even without the great aesthetic beauties, would make the film unique in the cinema of historical reconstruction.[100]

That same day, 16 December, was the New York première. *Lawrence* received a standing ovation. Afterwards, Lean fell into the company of David O. Selznick, who told him

They will do to you what they tried to do to me on *Gone With the Wind*. They will try to make you cut it. Don't let them. I refused to let them cut *Gone With the Wind* which they said was going to be hopeless if it wasn't cut because of the length – they could only get two shows a day. It's made more money than any film ever made. Don't let them touch *Lawrence*.[101]

Despite this authoritative advice, Lean continued to suspect that the film was too long.

New York was in the middle of a newspaper strike, so that only a few reviews made it into print, and most of those were hostile. Andrew Sarris of the *Village Voice* summed it up as 'dull, overlong and coldly impersonal … hatefully calculating and condescending.'[102] But the reviews on radio and television took quite a different line, while Lean, Spiegel, Sharif and O'Toole did their best to whip up interest by working the chat show circuits. Lean wrote to Barbara Cole that

Sam has just popped in to tell me that the NY box office is jammed with queues bigger than they've ever had … and that a TV personality has just gone on the air saying that anyone who misses *Lawrence* will be depriving himself of one of the greatest experiences of his life … And the Columbia stock has gone up from $14 to $25.[103]

The Los Angeles première was held on 21 December 1962. Lean reported that

The Hollywood audience was the best of the lot. They clapped two or three times but had an attentiveness far beyond London and New York. It was a sort of rave show and at the dinner afterwards it was rather wonderful because I knew that everyone present thought we had done something very substantial for the film medium.[104]

He elaborated on this reception in a letter to Bolt, in which his excitement sometimes overpowered his care for grammar:

... the reason that most film writers don't get credit is that they don't deserve it. Most so-called script writers are adapters and 'added dialogue' writers. The movies don't possess a dramatist. For that reason this film of ours has knocked the top film-makers sideways.

In short, they all say they have never seen anything like it. The top American movie-makers are more generous than anyone in the world, and they have given us their praise on a plate. Don't quite know how to describe it to you at this distance but among the real ravers are Willy Wyler, Billy Wilder, Fred Zinnemann, Richard Brooks, Joe Mankiewicz and the great old-timer, King Vidor. They are all so bloody generous that every one of them has said words to the effect, 'It's out of our class' and really mean it ...

This film has put me into a fantastic position and that a team consisting of you and I would be backed up to the hilt – bigger than anyone in this so-called industry ...[105]

Cuts

On 1 January 1963, Lean flew back to New York to discuss possible cuts with Spiegel. Both men agreed that the film would be all the better for being trimmed to three hours; neither could quite work out how to lose four reels'-worth of footage. Lean eventually drew up a list of twenty minutes of cuts to be passed on to Anne Coates. Then he went off on yet another publicity tour.

There were fifteen cuts in all:

1 Shot of the goggles following the motorcycle crash.
2 The entire sequence in the crypt of St Paul's.
3 The beginning of the scene in the map room in Cairo.
4 The entire sequence with Lawrence in the Officers' Mess.
5 The beginning of the dialogue between Murray and Dryden.
6 The night sequence as Lawrence prepares to ride to Aqaba, when Feisal asks him in whose name he rides.
7 The entry into Auda's camp at Wadi Rumm and the start of the subsequent tracking shot of the feast.
8 Part of the scene of Lawrence, Daud and Farraj in Sinai.
9 The start of the sequence with Lawrence, Allenby, Dryden and Brighton in the Officers' Club, plus the whip-pan shot from the same sequence.
10 Three sections of dialogue from the scene with Feisal and Bentley.
11 The entire fireside scene with Allenby and Brighton.
12 Brief shots of Ali in Deraa as Lawrence is tortured.
13 Two sections of dialogue from the terrace scene with Allenby and Lawrence.
14 Brief dialogue between Auda, Bentley and Ali as Lawrence returns to the desert with his bodyguard.
15 A section of dialogue from the military briefing with Allenby.[106]

Awards

Lean returned to the United States in time for the Academy Awards on 8 April 1963; the venue was the Civic Auditorium, Santa Monica. *Lawrence* had been nominated for no fewer than ten Oscars; like Lean and Spiegel's previous film, *Kwai*, it took seven.

Best Picture: Sam Spiegel
Best Director: David Lean
Best Achievement in Cinematography: Freddie Young
Best Art Direction and Set Decoration: John Box, John Stoll, Dario Simoni

Best Achievement in Sound: John Cox and Shepperton Sound
    Department
Best Musical Score: Maurice Jarre
Best Achievement in Film Editing: Anne Coates.

There was considerable surprise that no Oscars were
forthcoming for O'Toole, Sharif or Bolt. Lean, who had been
annoyed by O'Toole's drunken behaviour on talk shows, had little
sympathy for his star, but

... the night was almost ruined for me by the fact that Robert and Omar
missed out ... I blame Sam and Columbia almost entirely for Robert's [failure
to take the expected prize] because he was entered in the category for scripts
from another source – which I think is quite wrong. *Freud* was listed as
original, and if that's original, surely *Lawrence* is too.[107]

The creative, financial and logistical struggles to bring
Lawrence to the screen had ended. Its makers could legitimately hope
to bask for a while in the agreeable waves of success. Instead, a new
set of morale-draining battles were already under way; battles that
were to be fought both in print and in the law courts of several
nations, and not to be fully settled for many years.

The writer

Michael Wilson, who was understandably curious as to how much
of his contribution had survived, asked Spiegel to let him see a copy
of Bolt's screenplay. Surprisingly, Spiegel complied. Wilson's
conclusion, as he wrote to Spiegel shortly afterwards, was that
though he was happy to concede that Bolt had made enormous
improvements to his dialogue,[108] the overall structure of the film
was his. In short, he deserved and demanded a joint credit with
Bolt. Wilson then wrote directly to Bolt, outlining the history
of his involvement with the project, his status as a blacklisted
writer, and the nature of his grievances.[109] He ended by threatening

to turn the matter over to the British Television and Screenwriters' Guild.

Bolt's reply to Wilson is dated 3 December 1962: 'Your letter this morning came as a bombshell. I had no idea that there was any question of my sharing credit with anybody. I was under the impression that the script as shot was my own work utterly …'

He went on to argue that, since both of them had taken their narrative line from *Seven Pillars*, Wilson had no claim to invention:

The exceptions are: the death of Daud by quicksand rather than by illness, and the collapsing of the two characters (the one whose life he saved in the Nefud and the one whose life he took to avoid tribal bloodshed) into one. I can't quite remember, but I know Sam and David told me one of these ideas was theirs, not yours, and I think they said both. In any event I can't agree that even both of these ideas would entitle you to equal billing as against the entire bulk of the script. I cannot tell you how hard I have worked on this film. Some of it I have written five times over to meet the requirements of Sam and David. It has been back-breaking and the target, for me, has been that it should be my script that is shot, and I think it is.

I wish you well; I have heard nothing but good things of you from people I respect; I am particularly sympathetic because of your particular political predicament; I have myself no objection to your receiving credit for 'preliminary work' or 'ideas' which are yours. But I'm damned if the screenplay is by anyone but Robert Bolt and that is what the Credit ought to say.[110]

The issue, as Wilson had threatened, went to an arbitration committee of the Writers' Guild. They reached their verdict in June 1963. Their unanimous vote went to Wilson; and several months later, on 18 December 1963, the Writers' Guild presented Wilson with the Award for Best Screenplay of 1962.

Bolt was disgusted by the whole business, and refused to speak to the press, instead writing a public statement. Of the several points he made to undermine Wilson's right to a credit, the most telling drew on an unlikely source: Professor A. W. Lawrence, the man who had been doing most to discredit the historical and psychological accuracy of Lean's film.

The Professor

A. W. Lawrence had not seen any of Bolt's script until July 1962, when all but three of the scenes were in the camera. He was appalled by what he saw as its distortions, and contacted his lawyer. On 7 August the lawyer told Lawrence that Spiegel was still keen to call his film *Seven Pillars of Wisdom*, but that if Lawrence exercised his right of veto over the title, he would have to forfeit the last £5,000 of his contract. By 16 August, Lawrence had decided that he would go ahead with the veto, and the money went back to Horizon Pictures. Spiegel, seeking to build bridges, invited Lawrence to see a rough assembly of the film.

Lawrence refused, but was then persuaded by his publisher that it might be wise to see how the script had turned out, so on 5 September, he and his wife Barbara went to the cutting rooms in South Audley Street. The reaction was predictable. Lean:

Lawrence was furious ... You felt the seats were heaving about five minutes before the end. He stood up and shouted at Sam, 'I should never have trusted you!' There was a horrendous row and he stormed out with his wife in pursuit, trying to placate him.[111]

On 16 December 1962, Professor Lawrence's article 'The Fiction and the Fact' was published in *The Observer*. Among its most telling points:

The film ... is above all a spectacle in which skilful directing, visual splendour and music sugar-coat the script's bitter treatment of character and events ...

The film Lawrence has more than any one man's share of psychological aberrations, which are displayed by episodes that do not appear in the book and by distorted versions of some that do ...

The real key to the hero is sadism – a trait which a good many Englishmen could have observed in T. E. Lawrence if it had existed ...

I do not want to give the impression that I consider the Lawrence of the film entirely untrue. So far especially as determination, courage and endurance are concerned, he is comparable, in Mr O'Toole's rendering, with the man he purports to represent. How much else is right or wrong, and how much of the truth, both good and bad, is missing, I must leave to people who are familiar with the relevant books. I need only say that I should not have recognised my brother.[112]

It is striking that the quality Professor Lawrence should have chosen as most offensive was 'sadism', since, as those most closely involved with the dispute were most aware, the truly alarming point for A. W. Lawrence was TE's penchant for masochistic practices. These were not made known to the general public until the late 1960s, with the publication of *The Secret Lives of Lawrence of Arabia*, but Anthony Nutting had already uncovered the family secret as part of his researches for the film:

What appeared on the screen was a very muted version of what I put in my book [*Lawrence of Arabia: The Man and the Motive*], where I called a spade a spade and said that Lawrence became a physical and emotional masochist ... There is considerable evidence that he enjoyed being flogged. That, of course, did not come out in the film, but there is a sort of muted element in the way he reacted to questions about his suffering in the desert and the agonies he went through.[113]

A. W. Lawrence was interviewed by the *New York Times*: he noted Bolt's involvement with CND, and said that in his view Bolt had written the script as anti-war propaganda. Given the right to reply, Bolt 'denied the film reflected his own disarmament beliefs by portraying a military leader as a maniac willing to sacrifice helpless and innocent people.' But he was swift to pick up on an aspect of the family's objections to his screenplay which considerably strengthened his case against Michael Wilson. 'Professor Lawrence', Bolt explained, 'T. E.'s brother and executive, publicly rejected my interpretation on the ground that it was radically different from that of Mr Wilson which he had previously approved.'[114]

Objections to the film came from others who claimed that their forebears had been travestied. The Allenby family made a formal complaint to Columbia; descendants of both Auda Abu Tayi and Sherif Ali initiated legal actions. As Nutting had predicted, Sherif Ali's family were angered by the killing in the 'mirage' scene; the case was dropped when Columbia's attorneys argued that the film clearly shows Ali firing in self-defence. The Auda Abu Tayi case was not so quickly settled. Auda's son argued that his father had been portrayed as a venal man, interested only in money and bribes – not quite the case, but not wholly without foundation, either. The dispute dragged on until the 1970s.

Bolt was disturbed by all these expressions of hostility, and proposed to his publishers, Heinemann, that when the screenplay was published it should be accompanied by a short essay of

Quinn as Auda

explanation. On 21 January 1963: Bolt delivered his 'Apologia', as he now called it, to his editor Edward Thompson, but he withdrew it just four days later. Lean, who was infuriated by the whole idea of apologising for their work, had written Bolt a firm letter suggesting that he should drop the essay.

The Apologia remained unpublished until Adrian Turner provided the text as an appendix to *Robert Bolt: Scenes from Two Lives* (1998), where it runs to five full pages. A good half of the text addresses the indignation that massacre sequence had provoked in Professor Lawrence and others. As telling evidence against those who maintained that TE took no active part in the slaughter, he cites the precise words of *Seven Pillars* (1926), Chapter CXVII, on which his treatment was founded: 'In a madness born of the horror of Tafas we killed and killed, even blowing in the heads of the fallen and the animals …'; 'I said, "The best of you brings me the most Turkish dead," and we turned after the fading enemy, on our way shooting down those who had fallen out by the roadside, and came imploring our pity …' and so on.

His remarks on the dramatic necessity of having certain individual characters represent ideas as much as individuals are persuasive, though not so much as to calm all objection:

For the unique circumstances [of TE's acts, both heroic and barbaric] complex military and political forces were responsible. These simplified and contracted to the range of half a dozen characters I made the background to his story in the sense of plot. Thus Ali has to represent emergent Arab nationalism, Dryden represents European political skills, Feisal the opposing skill of the native people. Allenby is the one appointed to power, through whom Dryden must work. The present Lady Allenby has been shocked by my portrayal of this very considerable man. I want to say that as I wrote the part I admired him exceedingly and tried to show him as performing his duty – the duty given him by us, his people – perfectly and without relish. A weakness of historical drama is that individuals who could fairly claim to have been the instruments of impersonal forces must be made unreally conscious of their role in order that they may express it. (Consider that magnificent, necessary and implausible soliloquy of Gloucester's at the opening of Richard.) And thus, vis-à-vis the Arabs, the duplicity of British policy appears here like Allenby's own. Vis-à-vis Lawrence, the ruthlessness enjoined upon a field commander – our ruthlessness – looks like his.[115]

His conclusion:

... in a deeper sense than that of plot, the background to the story is the Desert. Words cannot trap that landscape; the camera almost can, and did. It is the essence of the saga. The aesthete in Lawrence revelled in its fantasy and almost luscious colourings. The stoic in him bit hard on its inhumanities. And it was alien; he alone was in it. We tried to show, in short, a man awkward among his own, accepted by an alien people, but accepted by them as something he was not – 'posturing', as he says, 'in borrowed robes' – and not as a man among others but as a heaven sent leader. Thus he had the power, and no mores to guide him in the use of it.

That is the theme which I thought I found in Seven Pillars and tried to deploy in this filmscript ...[116]

Heinemann began to have cold feet about the Lawrence affair. To this day, there has been no British edition of the screenplay.

The next three decades saw further revisions and additions to the Lawrence myth, while the movie developed from being simply one lavish box-office success among many to the status of established classic: indeed, a regular candidate for the title of Greatest Film Ever Made. Many of those involved in its making died in the interim; but Lean remained alive and vigorous enough to oversee the next, unforeseen chapter in his film's fate.

7 Reputation and Restoration: 1962–2007

All men dream; but not equally. Those who dream by night in the dusty recesses of their minds wake in the day to find that it was vanity: but the dreamers of the day are dangerous men, for they may act their dream with open eyes, to make it possible. This I did.

TE, *Seven Pillars of Wisdom*

Brief updates

Peter O'Toole's subsequent movie career has often been busy. His finest moments after *Lawrence* were mainly in comedies: *My Favorite Year* (1982) on film, and *Jeffrey Bernard Is Unwell* on stage and television; but none of these roles has had the daemonic intensity of his part in *Lawrence*. He habitually refuses interviews about his work with Lean; his well-reviewed autobiographies have not yet reached the events of 1961–2.

Omar Sharif took the lead role in the next Lean–Bolt collaboration, *Doctor Zhivago* (1965). Like O'Toole, he went on to appear in dozens of films. Like O'Toole, he has never equalled the global impact of his role in *Lawrence*, and has been better known as a sophisticated hedonist – a world-class bridge player – than as a dramatic artist.

Alec Guinness became unexpectedly wealthy late in life as a result of his brief but dignified appearance as Obi-Wan Kenobi in *Star Wars* (1977), for which he took two and a half per cent of profits. He appeared both in *Doctor Zhivago* and in Lean's last film, *A Passage to India* (1984), but the most memorable role of his later years was probably that of John Le Carré's lugubrious cuckold George Smiley in *Tinker, Tailor, Soldier, Spy* (1979) and subsequent adaptations from the Smiley series.

Claude Rains died in 1967.

Jack Hawkins died in 1973.

Robert Bolt became the highest-paid screenwriter of his generation. The visible part of his long-term collaborations with Lean comprises just two more films: *Doctor Zhivago* – for which he won an Oscar – and *Ryan's Daughter* (1970); the invisible part, two screenplays on the subject of the *Bounty* mutiny, *The Lawbreakers* (1978) and *The Long Arm* (1979), plus an adaptation of Joseph Conrad's *Nostromo* (1989). Roger Donaldson took over the two mutiny scripts as the basis for *The Bounty* (1984). The most successful of Bolt's scripts for other directors was *The Mission* (1986; directed by Roland Joffe.) He made one attempt at directing his own work, *Lady Caroline Lamb*: a conspicuous failure. His private life was often troubled. In 1979 he suffered a major stroke which left him partially paralysed and with impaired speech, though with quite unimpaired intelligence. He died in 1995.

Sam Spiegel went on to produce some interesting work, though nothing to rival his collaborations with Lean: *The Chase* (1966) directed by Arthur Penn and starring Marlon Brando, Jane Fonda, and Robert Redford; *The Night of the Generals* (1967), which re-united O'Toole and Sharif; *Nicholas and Alexandra* (1969), which looked to many like a pallid pastiche of Lean's epic style; *The Last Tycoon* (1976), from the novel by F. Scott Fitzgerald, with Robert De Niro and Jack Nicholson; and, finally, *Betrayal* (1982), from a script by Harold Pinter. He died on New Year's Eve, 1985.

Michael Wilson died of a heart attack in 1978, at the age of sixty-three. His last years had been damaged by heavy drinking, and he only achieved three more screen credits, one for *Planet of the Apes* (adapted from a novel by, of all authors, Pierre Boulle) and another, closer to his radical heart, for *Che* (1969). After his death, the cause of the *Lawrence* credit was taken up by his brother-in-law Paul Jarrico, and came to a renewed head in 1989, at the time of the film's restoration. Wilson's name was still missing from the credits of the restored film, but in the summer of 1995 Columbia eventually agreed to include it in all subsequent theatrical releases and DVDs. To date, they have been true to this agreement.

A. W. Lawrence finally made a public statement about his older brother's sexuality in 1986 when interviewed by Julia Cave for her BBC documentary *Lawrence and Arabia*:

He hated the thought of sex. He had read any amount of mediaeval literature about characters – some of them saints, some of them not – who had quelled sexual longings by beatings. And that's what he did. I knew about it immediately after his death, but of course said nothing. It's not a thing people can understand easily.[117]

Professor Lawrence died in 1991. His obituarist in *The Times* noted that 'He dissociated himself from [Lean's film] ... not from a desire to conceal the truth but from a concern to see such subjects discussed seriously, not sensationally.'

David Lean's life was radically transformed by *Lawrence*: he was now widely regarded as one of the world's leading directors. In the words of William Goldman, writing in 1983:

A rule of mine is this: there are always three hot directors and one of them is always David Lean. Today it's Lucas, Spielberg and Lean. A few years back Coppola, Friedkin and Lean. A few years before that, Penn, Nichols and Lean.[118]

Yet his output in the years after *Lawrence* was slender: just three completed films – *Zhivago, Ryan's Daughter, A Passage to India* – and with a gap of fourteen years between the latter two, and a six-year hiatus between the last and his death. Some of this apparently blank period was devoted to setting up projects that were never realised – the *Bounty* films, *Nostromo* – and some of it was due to the increasing difficulty of making films on a colossal scale at a time when blockbusters often performed poorly and low-budget films (from *Easy Rider* to *Saturday Night Fever*) were vastly profitable. In this climate, Lean was highly respected but virtually unbankable.

But another reason for his withdrawal into cosseted and itinerant non-productiveness, as Kevin Brownlow has detailed in his major biography, was a crisis of confidence. *Ryan's Daughter* had drawn some of the worst reviews of Lean's career, and the experience of public humiliation was rendered unbearable by an evening in New York which Lean later described as 'one of the most horrible experiences I have ever had.'[119] Always nervous and distrustful of 'intellectuals', Lean suddenly found himself trapped in a room full of the species – members of the National Society of Film Critics, including Pauline Kael and Richard Schickel. It was, in effect, a verbal mugging.

As Lean remembered the evening, Richard Schickel was one of the most vicious attackers – a version Schickel disputes, though he does recall trying to give the meeting focus with a rather infelicitous summary – 'What they're trying to say, Mr Lean, is that they don't understand how someone who made *Brief Encounter* could make a piece of bullshit like *Ryan's Daughter*.'[120] Lean retreated into silence, and for days afterwards was in a state of shock.

I thought, 'What the hell am I doing if my work is as bad as all this?' I didn't want to do another film, I thought, 'I'll do something else.' I went travelling around the world and didn't make a film for fourteen years. I thought, 'What's the point?'[121]

This is misleading. However stunned he might have been, Lean spent a good part of the next year trying to revive an old project, *Gandhi*; and he was inspired by the story of Captain Cook, which might have formed part of a South Pacific trilogy with the two *Bounty* films. Lean was knighted in October 1984, just a few weeks before the Los Angeles world première of *A Passage to India*. The American critics received the film rapturously – in some cases, sheepishly aware of the part they had played in chasing Lean from the screen. The last great public triumph of his life would be the restoration of *Lawrence* in 1989. He died on 16 April 1991.

T. E. Lawrence's reputation continues to undergo radical changes, and the fascination he holds for us has, if anything, grown since 1962. (An exhibition devoted to his life and legend at London's Imperial War Museum in 2006 was so crammed with visitors that one was obliged to queue for up to an hour or more, and then to shuffle, not walk, through the displays.)[122] The publication in 1969 of a bestselling biography, *The Secret Lives of Lawrence of Arabia* (Knightley and Simpson) made public the fact that Lawrence had arranged for one of his fellow servicemen to flog him regularly. The masochism – if that is the exact term – which A. W. Lawrence had struggled to keep a family secret now became one of the single best-known components of the Lawrence myth.

A longer, far more sympathetic and thoughtful biography of TE, *A Prince of Our Disorder*, was published in 1976. The work of an eminent scholar, John Mack – then Professor of Psychology at Harvard – this was the first major attempt to view Lawrence's life and career through the lens of psychoanalytic method. Surprisingly, the effect of Mack's book was not to debunk what was left of TE's reputation after the hostile assessments of Aldington (1955) and company, but to restore and even elevate it. It was not until 1989 that the first authorised biography appeared: Jeremy Wilson's *Lawrence of Arabia*. Further biographies have been appearing at intervals, and will surely continue to appear.

Criticisms of TE's career from political viewpoints began in earnest with Suleiman Mousa's *T. E. Lawrence: An Arab View*, published in English translation in 1966. This hostile but measured and well-informed debunking has been followed by attacks from a number of ideological positions, including Elie Koudrie's passionately anti-Arab essay 'The Real T. E. Lawrence' in *Commentary*, July 1977, and Edward Said's no less passionately pro-Arab offensive in his bestselling *Orientalism* (1978). Many people have been impressed by Said's book, including some film critics.[123] A salutary account of the shortcomings of Said's vision of TE can be found in Robert Irwin's *For Lust of Knowing: The Orientalists and Their Enemies* (2006), Chapter 9.

The only substantial dramatic work about Lawrence to appear since Lean's was the dull television film *A Dangerous Man: Lawrence after Arabia* (1992), produced by David Puttnam and starring Ralph Fiennes. It deals mainly with the post-war period of diplomacy in Paris, and its title comes from a well-known passage near the beginning of *Seven Pillars of Wisdom*, cited at the head of this chapter. An odd detail: this same passage was used as an end title for the final episode of Roseanne Barr's long-running situation comedy *Roseanne*.

Lawrence's most recent re-entry to the world's consciousness came with the announcement that the military forces of the USA and UK serving in Iraq (a country which TE had a hand in creating during the post-war negotiations over the fate of the Middle East) had been issued with Lawrence's advisory document of 1917, which outlines the best ways of working with Arab forces.[124] As long as the conflicts in the Middle East persist, Lawrence's ghost will continue to return.

Restoration

The man behind the scheme to restore the full original cut of *Lawrence of Arabia* was Robert A. Harris, the director of a distribution company called Images Film Archive. Harris had worked with Tom Luddy, from Francis Ford Coppola's Zoetrope company, on a warmly received restoration of Abel Gance's *Napoléon* (1927). There were two sets of cuts to set about amending: those made shortly after the 1962 première, and a second set of trims made in 1970 when the film was first released for television screenings, which reduced the 1962 running time of 222 minutes to 187 minutes.

The search for missing footage began in the summer of 1986, with the support of Dennis Doph, the head of Columbia Classics. Then David Puttnam became President and CEO: a fan of Lean's film, he asked if it could be ready in time for the next Cannes festival

– five months away. But the task was harder than anyone had imagined, since it was assumed that no one had ever touched the camera negative. On the contrary: it had been cut twice, with no adequate records of how the cuts had been made.

Harris's luck improved when he discovered that Anne Coates – apart from Lean himself, the person best qualified to work on the project – was cutting a film in the next building to his own. In January 1987, a lorry delivered some 4,000 pounds of assorted negative cuts and trims to Harris's office. A month or so of searching yielded about ten minutes of lost scenes, albeit in dirty condition and on black-and-white stock. Then Lean – regarded with awe by Harris – came to see what they were doing; was fired with enthusiasm; and joined in the restoration process, but in a more radical way than Harris had intended. He saw his chance to set right some points which had long nagged at him: for example, he was able to give a different tone to the blood-bath sequence by showing Lawrence gazing in horror at the bodies of women and children murdered by the retreating Turks.

Things were going nicely until March 1987, when Columbia got wind of the fact that someone appeared to be in the process of making money from company property, demanded changes to their deal with Harris and, in effect, closed the restoration down. Puttnam tried to help, but soon afterwards was fired. His replacement, Dawn Steel, was also a fan of Lean's work, and allowed Harris to start again. Martin Scorsese and Steven Spielberg were recruited, ensuring that any further opposition from Columbia would seem philistine, and Anne Coates began cutting again.

One of the problems they faced was that eight minutes of recovered footage had no soundtrack at all. Harris called on lip-readers to work out what was being said, and re-recorded dialogue with Arthur Kennedy and Anthony Quinn. In London, Lean supervised recordings with O'Toole and Guinness. All of these contributions had to be treated electronically to disguise the change of vocal tone wrought by three and a half decades.

Problems continued. Though the original negative had been re-humidified to make it pliable, it had dried out again during the intervening months, and in February 1988, Harris discovered that the splices simply fell apart. Eventually, though, the restored *Lawrence* was ready for its first public screenings in Washington, New York and Los Angeles in 1989. Harris and his colleagues warned Lean that American audiences were no longer the respectful, attentive kind he had known in the early 1960s, but the warnings were needless. Audiences were rapt, silent. Notices were rapturous. Some said it was the most impressive film they had ever seen.

Lean's speech at the New York première was unexpectedly revealing:

Lawrence was to young English boys [of my generation] the last word in exotic heroes. We saw pictures of him in that exotic dress and headgear. We heard Lowell Thomas sing his praises over the radio. But then Lawrence is an enigma and I've always been fond of enigmas. I liked the 'flawed heroes'. Perfection is dull. When I was a boy, I would pick on the most eccentric person in the room and study him.[125]

The informal triumph of the re-release was soon to be consolidated by formal recognition. On 8 March 1990, the American

12 February 1989:
Spielberg, Scorsese et al.
celebrate the *Lawrence*
restoration

Film Institute gave Lean its Lifetime Achievement Award. Steven Spielberg delivered one of the keynote speeches:

David brought me here, and in fact you could say bought me my ticket. Because it was two of his films, *The Bridge on the River Kwai* and *Lawrence of Arabia*, that most made me want to be a film-maker. The scope and audacity of those films filled my dreams with unlimited possibilities. *Lawrence* gives me the same spark of inspiration now, and thanks to the restoration its inspiration can be, to all of us, perpetual.

We have to look back so that we can keep looking forward, and whenever I turn around I see only *Lawrence*. Every tool used to make movies was used in the making of *Lawrence of Arabia,* used and abused, sometimes past what we might have thought possible. The performances, the editing, the score, the costume design, the production design and Robert Bolt's screenplay which, as far as I'm concerned, is the best ever written, all these elements were put together by David Lean with consummate brilliance and absolute economy. There is nothing extraneous in *Lawrence* or in any Lean picture. There is nothing ever wasted. Every shot is a tool that unlocks the plot and every image an echo of the heart. So for me *Lawrence* is somewhere between a cornerstone and a grail.

I was inspired the first time I saw *Lawrence*. It made me feel puny. It still makes me feel puny. And that's just one measure of its greatness, because it's a continued inspiration and it's cutting the rest of us down to size ... [126]

Heartfelt as it is, this handsome tribute is somewhat misleading. The direct inspiration of *Lawrence* is, quite true, manifest in the films of Spielberg, and of the few other directors who have been in a position to make epics. In the years since *Heaven's Gate* sank a studio, however, epics on grown-up subjects have been an endangered breed. (Epic fantasies are quite a different matter.) None the less, the distant reverberations of *Lawrence* may be heard in a surprisingly wide range of movies: *Apocalypse Now*[127] (1979), *The Last Emperor* (1987), *Malcolm X*[128], *The English Patient* ... and *Star Wars*?

Envoi

This is in danger of becoming a merely triumphalist ending; and Lawrence was being mordantly ironic when he called *Seven Pillars of Wisdom* 'A Triumph'. *Lawrence of Arabia* also shuns triumphalism, and – as noted at the outset – is in effect a version of tragedy. In its last scene we see (or more exactly: half-see: recall the ploy of making Lawrence more and more intangible from the last scene with Allenby onwards: here, he is partly concealed by a dusty windscreen) the newly appointed Colonel Lawrence being driven off to the ship that will take him back to England. 'Well, Sir, goin' 'ome,' says his cockney driver (Bryan Pringle). We know, as the driver does not, that Lawrence is a man without a tribe or a nation. He has no 'home'.

The car passes a group of Arabs on camels: a memento of what he will be missing. A solo motorcyclist passes them – a delicate, but telling reminder of the death that lies waiting implacably for him, seventeen years in the future. But this is a modern tragedy, not a Shakespearean one, and Lawrence is dead only in spirit, not in flesh. It was TE himself who – thinking of the life and death of Sir Roger Casement[129] – devised the phrase which best designates his condition in this final shot.

He is a broken archangel.

Notes

1 Brown (ed.), *Letters*, (Oxford: Oxford University Press, 1988; republished 1991), p. 289.

2 Including some of the critics I most admire: David Thomson, for example, in his invaluable *Biographical Dictionary of Film*.

3 Byzantine general, c. AD 505–565; his career is recounted by his secretary Procopius in *The Secret History*. Legend has it that Belisarius ended up as a beggar, and the resonance of this myth in TE's life did not escape his friends. See Robert Graves's poem 'The Stater'.

4 Brown (ed.), *Letters*, p. 511.

5 Cited in Philip Hoare, *Noel Coward*, p. 225. TE is often thought of as painfully solemn, but he thought this very funny: see Brown (ed.), *Letters*, p. 443.

6 See his letter to Lionel Curtis, 19 March 1923; Brown (ed.), *Letters*, p. 227.

7 TE quipped about this himself: see David Garnett, *The Familiar Faces*, p. 104.

8 See Brown (ed.), *Letters*, p. 178 n.

9 Though quite a bit is adumbrated for those with sharp eyes and ears. Note, for example, the moment when Lawrence spots an unfamiliar antiquity in the Cairo Arab Bureau.

10 Cited in Adrian Turner, *Robert Bolt: Scenes from Two Lives* (London: Hutchinson, 1998), p. 187.

11 Lean sometimes lamented that he had not had the nerve to make more of the film seem like a Dali landscape: see Kevin Brownlow, *David Lean* (London: Faber, 1996), p. 437: '... we get scared because these damnable rules of "reality" jump up and censor our imaginations.'

12 TE's linguistic abilities are better summed up as 'competent'. By the end of the war, he had a vocabulary of about 12,000 words, but his syntax was wobbly, and, according to Harry St John Philby, his accent was poor. Feisal described listening to TE's Arabic as 'a perpetual adventure'. See Lawrence James, *The Golden Warrior* (London: Abacus Books, 1990), p. 365.

13 Cited in James, *Golden Warrior*, p. 294.

14 T. E. Lawrence, *Seven Pillars of Wisdom* (Harmondsworth: Penguin, 1926), pp. 532–3.

15 'In my saddle-bags was a *Morte d'Arthur*. It relieved my disgust. The men had only physical resources ...': Lawrence, *Seven Pillars*.

16 The words of Hippocleides, who had successfully wooed princess Agarista, but then disgraced himself by getting drunk and dancing upside-down, thus revealing his genitals. 'You have danced away your wife,' said her father. Hippocleides replied that he did not care.

17 Lawrence was an expert rider, but he had crashed a number of times before, usually when swerving to avoid some bird or animal. Though suicide is an unlikely verdict, it has plausibly been suggested that TE might have been in a mood of greater recklessness and personal neglect than usual. The recently retired are noted to be accident-prone.

18 Wilson's first screenplay had been much more directly based on the *Kane* overture.

19 In *T. E. Lawrence by His Friends*, ed. A. W. Lawrence (1937, revised 1954), p. 165.

20 Cited in James, *Golden Warrior*, p. 442.

21 James, *Golden Warrior*, p. 443.

22 James, *Golden Warrior*, p. 435.

23 James, *Golden Warrior*, p. 9.

24 James, *Golden Warrior*, p. 404.

25 Cited in James, *Golden Warrior*, p. 450.

26 Cited in John Mack, *A Prince of Our Disorder*, p. 492. From C. S. Jarvis, *Three Deserts*, 1936.

27 Cited in Mack, *A Prince of Our Disorder*, p. 442.

28 Brown (ed.), *Letters*, p. 482.

29 Discussions of heroism in the interwar years were often dominated by the figure of Lawrence, both directly and in fictional versions. W. H. Auden addressed the TE myth in both prose and poetry; the Marxist Christopher Caudwell analysed him in terms of dying bourgeois civilisation; the young André Malraux idolised him …

30 Herbert Wilcox, *Twenty-Five Thousand Sunsets* (London: Bodley Head, 1967), p. 204.

31 Cited in Andrew Kelly, Jeffrey Richards and James Pepper, *Filming T. E. Lawrence: Korda's Lost Epics* (London: I. B. Tauris, 1997), p. 2.

32 See R. Bullard, *The Camels Must Go*, p. 158.

33 Mack, *Prince of Our Disorder*, p. 393; TE to Ede, 18 October 1932, in *Shaw-Ede: T. E. Lawrence's Letters to H. S. Ede, 1927–1935* (1942), p. 54.

34 Mack, *Prince of Our Disorder*, p. 393; from Weintraub, *Private Shaw and Public Shaw*, p. 227.

35 Wilson, *Twenty-five Thousand Sunsets*, p. 916.

36 Brown (ed.), *Letters*, p. 489.

37 Brown (ed.), *Letters*, p. 490.

38 Brown (ed.), *Letters*, p. 493.

39 Brown (ed.), *Letters*, p. 498.

40 Brown (ed.), *Letters*, pp. 515–16.

41 Mack, *Prince of Our Disorder*, p. 404; from Reginald Sims, 'The Sayings and Doings of T.E. as Heard and Experienced by the Sims Family' (1937); private collection.

42 Brown (ed.), *Letters*, p. 520.

43 Brownlow, *David Lean*, p. 406.

44 For a text of the Malleson/Hurst/Guthrie script, dated 4 October 1938, see Kelly *et al.*, *Filming T. E. Lawrence*, pp. 31–129.

45 Interview with J. Danvers Williams in *Film Weekly*, 20 November 1937. The full text is reprinted in Kelly *et al.*, *Filming T. E. Lawrence*, pp. 22–7.

46 Cited in Kelly, *et al.*, *Filming T. E. Lawrence*, p. 8.

47 Cited in Kelly, *et al.*, *Filming T. E. Lawrence*, p. 8.

48 Cited in Kelly, *et al.*, *Filming T. E. Lawrence*, p. 10.

49 Cited in Kelly, *et al.*, *Filming T. E. Lawrence*, p. 14.

50 Cited in Kelly, *et al.*, *Filming T. E. Lawrence*, pp. 14–15.

51 Cited in Kelly, *et al.*, *Filming T. E. Lawrence*, p. 17.

52 Adrian Turner, *The Making of 'Lawrence of Arabia'* (LImpsfield, Surrey: Dragon's World, 1994), pp. 31–2.

53 Cited in Brownlow, *David Lean*, p. 407.

54 Wilson, *The Outsider* (Los Angeles, CA), p. 71. See also William M. Chace's 'T. E. Lawrence: The Uses of Heroism' in Jeffrey Meyers (ed.), *T. E. Lawrence: Soldier, Writer, Legend* (London: Macmillan, 1989).

55 Cited in Brownlow, *David Lean*, p. 408.

56 This is almost certainly a gross exaggeration.

57 Cited in Brownlow, *David Lean*, p. 421.

58 Cited in Brownlow, *David Lean*, p. 423.

59 Cited in Brownlow, *David Lean*, p. 424.

60 Turner, *Making*, p. 82.

61 Cited in Brownlow, *David Lean*, p. 433.

62 Cited in Brownlow, *David Lean*, p. 433.

63 Published in the *New York Times*, 15 May 1961.

64 Cited in Brownlow, *David Lean*, p. 429.

65 Not, that is, 65mm rushes. Peter Newbrook recalls – Brownlow, *David Lean*, p. 451 – that Techicolor initially tried to send 35mm reduction prints out to the desert, but they were so poorly graded as to be useless for Lean's purposes. He resolved to carry on without them.

66 Cited in Turner, *Making*, p. 115.

67 Cited in Turner, *Making*, p. 119.

68 Cited in Brownlow, *David Lean*, p. 436.

69 Brownlow, *David Lean*, p. 436–7.

70 Browlow, *David Lean*, p. 437.

71 Cited in Turner, *Making*, pp. 121–2.

72 Turner, *Making*, p. 124.

73 Turner, *Making*, p. 131.

74 Cited in Turner, *Making*, pp. 124–5.

75 Turner, *Making*, p. 127; and see Brownlow, *David Lean*, p. 445.

76 Cited in Turner, *Robert Bolt*, p. 197; from Ronald Hayman, *Robert Bolt* (London: Heinemann, 1969), p. 14.

77 From Barber, p. 81.

78 Both citations in Turner, *Making*, p. 129.

79 Cited in Turner, *Making*, p. 129.

80 A substantial portion of the full text is given by Brownlow in *David Lean*, pp. 453–6.

81 Brownlow, *David Lean*, p. 455.

82 Brownlow, *David Lean*, p. 456.

83 Brown (ed.), *Letters*, pp. 261–2.

84 Cited in Turner, *Robert Bolt*, p. 198; dated 16 October 1961.

85 Really? I have yet to meet anyone who did not understand quite well what was happening.

86 Cited in Brownlow, *David Lean*, p. 459.

87 Brownlow, *David Lean*, p. 471.

88 Turner, *Making*, pp. 140–1.

89 Turner, *Making*, p. 143.

90 Cited in Brownlow, *David Lean*, p. 464.

91 On the topic of TE as a kind of Kurtz, see Jeffrey Meyers, 'T. E. Lawrence in His Letters': 'Lawrence's letters portray him as a modern Kurtz, a tortured soul, an alienated and divided man ...'; Meyers, *T. E. Lawrence*, p. 9.

92 Turner, *Making*, p. 150.

93 Brownlow, *David Lean*, p. 474.

94 Brownlow, *David Lean*, p. 474.

95 Brown (ed.), *Letters*, p. 496.

96 Cited in Brownlow, *David Lean*, p. 479.

97 *The Observer*, 16 December 1962.

98 *New Statesman*, 14 December 1962.

99 *Evening Standard*, 13 December 1962.

100 *Sunday Times*, 16 December 1962.

101 Cited in Brownlow, *David Lean*, p. 482; from Lean interview.

102 *Village Voice*, 20 December 1962.

103 Letter dated 17 December 1962.

104 Letter to Robert Bolt, 23 December 1962.

105 Cited in Turner, *Robert Bolt*, pp. 214–15.

106 Turner, *Making*, p. 171.

107 Letter to Barbara Cole, 15 April 1963.

108 For an illustration of Bolt's improvements, see Turner, *Making*, pp. 53–7.

109 An extensive quotation from this letter is given in Brownlow, *David Lean*, p. 477.

110 Cited in Turner, *Robert Bolt*, pp. 210–11.

111 Cited in Turner, *Robert Bolt*, p. 202.

112 Cited in Turner, *Robert Bolt*, p. 203; from *The Observer*, 16 December 1962.

113 Cited in Brownlow, *David Lean*, pp. 475–6.

114 Cited in Turner, *Robert Bolt*, p. 212.

115 Cited in Turner, *Robert Bolt*, pp. 508–9.

116 Cited in Turner, *Robert Bolt*, p. 509.

117 Cited in Brownlow, *David Lean*, p. 476.

118 Cited in Sandra Lean, with Barry Chattington, *David Lean: An Intimate Portrait* (New York: Universe, 2001) p. 44.

119 Brownlow, *David Lean*, p. 586.

120 Brownlow, *David Lean*, p. 587.

121 Brownlow, *David Lean*, p. 588.

122 This was so, at any rate, on the days I attended.

123 See, for example, Ella Shohat's 'Gender and Culture of Empire: Toward a Feminist Ethnography of Cinema', *Quarterly Review of Film & Video*, vol. 13 (1991); and Steven C. Caton's '*Lawrence of Arabia*': A Film's Anthropology (Berkeley: University of California Press, 1999), *passim*.

124 See James, *Golden Warrior*, pp. 463–4.

125 Cited in Lean, *David Lean*, p. 20.

126 Cited in Lean, *David Lean*, p. 54.

127 Especially, perhaps, in its original screenplay by John Milius? Other films by Milius also echo *Lawrence*.

128 Spike Lee and his cinematographer Ernest Dickerson 'saw the restored version of *Lawrence of Arabia*. It was always one of our favourite films, but to see it on the big screen in 70mm for the first time really blew us away. The close-ups were so sharp, so immediate. We wanted to shoot *Malcolm X* in the same way': Dickerson, cited in *Spike Lee: That's My Story and I'm Sticking to It*, p. 158.

129 See Brown (ed.), *Letters*, p. 508. TE was almost certainly thinking of Lamb's description of Coleridge as an 'Arch angel, a little damaged'. See *The Letters of Charles and Mary Lamb* (1975), Vol. III, p. 215.

Credits

Lawrence of Arabia
Great Britain/USA 1962

Directed by
David Lean
Produced by
Sam Spiegel
Screenplay by
Robert Bolt
Michael Wilson*
Director of Photography
F. A. Young, B.S.C.
Editor
Anne V. Coates
Production designed by
John Box
Music composed by
Maurice Jarre

©1962. Horizon Pictures
(GB) Ltd
Production Companies
The Sam Spiegel – David
Lean production of ...
Produced by Horizon
Pictures (GB) Ltd
(London, England)
Released through
Columbia Pictures
Corporation

Production Manager
John Palmer
Location Manager
Douglas Twiddy
Second Unit Direction
Andre Smagghe
Noel Howard
Assistant Director
Roy Stevens

Continuity
Barbara Cole
Casting Director
Maude Spector
Camera Operator
Ernest Day
**Second Unit
Photography**
Skeets Kelly
Nicolas Roeg
Peter Newbrook
Chief Electrician
Archie Dansie
Special Effects
Cliff Richardson
Art Director
John Stoll
Assistant Art Directors
R. [Roy] Rossotti
G. [George] Richardson
T. [Terence] Marsh
A. [Anthony]
Rimmington
Set Dresser
Dario Simoni
Property Master
Eddie Fowlie
Construction Manager
Peter Dukelow
Construction Assistant
Fred Bennett
Costume Designer
Phyllis Dalton
Wardrobe
John Wilson-Apperson
Make-up
Charles Parker
Hairdresser
A. G. Scott

(Music) played by
The London
Philharmonic Orchestra
Conductor
Sir Adrian Boult
Orchestrations by
Gerard Schurmann
Sound Recording
Paddy Cunningham
Sound Dubbing
John Cox
Sound Editor
Winston Ryder
*Robert Bolt received sole
writing credit on original
prints of the film;
however a 1995 Writers'
Guild of America ruling
added Michael Wilson's
name to the credits and
subsequent prints reflect
this change.

CAST
Alec Guinness
Prince Feisal
Anthony Quinn
Auda Abu Tayi
Jack Hawkins
General Allenby
Jose Ferrer
Turkish Bey
Anthony Quayle
Colonel Harry Brighton
Claude Rains
Mr Dryden
Arthur Kennedy
Jackson E. Bentley
I. S. Johar
Gasim

Gamil Rattib
Majid
Zia Moyheddin
Tafas
Michel Ray
Farraj
John Dimech
Daud
and
Donald Wolfit
General Murray
with
Omar Sharif
as Sherif Ali ibn el
Kharish
introducing
Peter O'Toole
as T. E. Lawrence
**Howard Marion
Crawford**
medical officer
Jack Gwillim
club secretary
Hugh Miller
R. A. M. C. Colonel

*selected uncredited cast in
order of appearance*
Noel Howlett
vicar at St Paul's
Jack Hedley
reporter at St Paul's
Ian Macnaughton
Corporal Hartley,
map room

Harry Fowler
Corporal William Potter,
map room
John Barry
MP, map room
Bruce Beeby
Captain, Officers' Club
Patrick Kavanagh
Staff-Major, Murray's
aide
Norman Rossington
Corporal Jenkins
Henry Oscar
Selim, Koran reciter
John Ruddock
elder Harith
Kamal Rashid
Auda's son
David Lean
voice of motorcyclist,
Suez Canal
Roy Stevens
driver, Cairo
Fred Bennett
Sergeant, Cairo
Peter Dukelow
driver, Cairo
Cyril Shaps
bartender, Officers' Club
Daniel Moynihan
officer, Officers' Club
Robert Bolt
soldier with pipe,
Officers' Club
Fernando Sancho
Turkish sergeant
Clive Morton
Artillery General, field
briefing

John Robinson
Infantry General, field
briefing
Basil Dignam
Cavalry General, field
briefing
Mohammed Habachi
Talal
Cher Kaoiu
Khitan of Aleppo
Kenneth Fortescue
Tracey, Allenby's ADC
Peter Burton
sheik, Arab Council
Bryan Pringle
driver, end sequence

'The producers gratefully
acknowledge the co-
operation extended to
them by the Royal
Hashemite Government
of Jordan and the Royal
Government of Morocco'

'Photographed on
overseas locations
[Jordan, Spain and
Morocco] and completed
at Shepperton Studios
(Shepperton, England)'

Filmed from 15 May 1961
to 20 October 1962
Colour by Technicolor
Photographed in Super-
Panavision 70
RCA Sound Recording

UK distributor: Columbia Pictures through BLC.
Running time: 222 minutes
US distributor: Columbia Pictures. Running time: 222 minutes
The film was cut for its general release in 1963, and further cuts were made for the circa 1970 re-release.

Credits for the restoration
©1988. Horizon Pictures (GB), Ltd
Reconstructed and Restored by
Robert A. Harris
Restoration Produced by
Robert A. Harris
Jim Painten

Editorial Consultant
Anne V. Coates, A.C.E.
Sound Consultant
Richard L. Anderson, M.P.S.E.
Rerecording Mixer
Gregg Landaker
65mm Negative Restoration by
Metrocolor Laboratories
70mm Prints by
Metrocolor Laboratories
35mm Prints by
DeLuxe
Assistants
Jude Schneider
Maggie Field
Joanne Lawson
Special Thanks to
Martin Scorsese
Steven Spielberg
Jon Davison
and Sir David Lean

Dolby Stereo Spectral Recording
Rerecorded in Dolby 6 Track SR at Goldwyn Sound Facilities

Restoration version running time: 228 minutes 0 seconds (i.e. 216 minutes plus overture, entr'acte and exit music)

Credits compiled by Julian Grainger

Select Bibliography

The literature on T E. Lawrence is unreadably vast: the most recent bibliography runs to 600 pages, and fresh studies appear by the year, if not the month. For the sake of sanity, I have listed here only the books which contributed directly to my essay, or are for various reasons worth reading in their own right. Other references may be found in the Notes.

By Lawrence

Lawrence, T. E., *Crusader Castles* (London: Michael Haag, 1937; republished 1987).

——, *The Essential T. E. Lawrence*, edited by David Garnett (Oxford: Oxford University Press, 1951; republished 1992).

——, *Letters*, edited by David Garnett (London: The Reprint Society, 1938; republished 1941).

——, *Letters*, edited by Malcolm Brown (Oxford: Oxford University Press, 1988; republished 1991).

——, *Letters to His Biographers Robert Graves and Liddell Hart* (New York: Doubleday, 1938; republished 1963).

——, *Minorities*, edited by Jeremy Wilson (New York: Doubleday, 1972).

——, *The Mint* (Harmondsworth: Penguin, 1955; reprinted in unexpurgated form 1978).

——, *The Odyssey*, translated by T. E. Shaw (New York: Oxford University Press, 1932; republished 1991).

——, *Revolt in the Desert* (New York: Tess Press, 1926; republished 2004).

——, *Seven Pillars of Wisdom* (Harmondsworth: Penguin, 1926 and 1935; republished 1962).

——, *Seven Pillars of Wisdom: The Complete 1922 Text* (Fordingbridge, Hampshire: J & N Wilson, 2004).

About Lawrence

Aldington, Richard, *Lawrence of Arabia, A Biographical Enquiry* (London: Collins, 1955).

Asher, Michael, *Lawrence, The Uncrowned King of Arabia* (London: Viking, 1998).

Barr, James, *Setting the Desert on Fire* (London: Bloomsbury, 2006}.

Bennett, Alan, *Forty Years On* (London: Faber, 1969).

Blackmur, R. P., *The Expense of Greatness*, (Gloucester, MA: Peter Smith, 1940; republished 1958).

Brown, Malcolm, *Lawrence of Arabia: The Life, the Legend* (London: Thames & Hudson, 2005).

Caudwell, Christopher, *Studies and Further Studies in a Dying Culture* (New York:,1938; republished 1971).

Graves, Robert, *Lawrence and the Arabs* (London: Cape, 1928).

Howe, Irving, *A World More Attractive* (New York: Horizon, 1963).

Irwin, Robert, *For Lust of Knowing: The Orientalists and Their Enemies* (London: Allen Lane, 2006).

James, Lawrence, *The Golden Warrior* (London: Abacus Books, 1990, 1995; republished 2005).

Knightley, Philip and Colin Simpson, *The Secret Lives of Lawrence of Arabia* (London: Panther Books, 1969; republished 1971).

Liddell Hart, B. H., *T. E. Lawrence: In Arabia and After* (London: Cape, 1934; republished 1965).

Mack, John, *A Prince of Our Disorder* (Cambridge, MA: Harvard University Press, 1976; republished 1998).

Meyers, Jeffrey, *The Wounded Spirit: A Study of Seven Pillars of Wisdom* (London: Martin Brian & O'Keeffe, 1973).

Meyers, Jeffrey (ed.), *T. E. Lawrence: Soldier, Writer, Legend* (London: Macmillan, 1989).

Mousa, Suleiman, *T. E. Lawrence: An Arab View*, trans. Albert Boutros (Oxford: Oxford University Press, 1966).

Nutting, Anthony, *Lawrence of Arabia: The Man and the Motive* (London: Hollis & Carter, 1961).

Ocampo, Victoria, *338171 T. E. Lawrence of Arabia*, trans. David Garnett (London: Gollancz, 1963).

Rattigan, Terence, *Ross: A Play in Two Acts* (London: Samuel French, 1960).

Richards, Vyvyan, *T. E. Lawrence* (London: Duckworth, 1939).

Said, Edward, *Orientalism* (Harmondsworth: Penguin, 1978; rev. edn 1995).

Thomas, Lowell, *With Lawrence in Arabia* (London: Hutchinson, 1924).

Wilson, Colin, *The Outsider* (London: Gollancz, 1956).

Wilson, Jeremy, *Lawrence of Arabia: The Authorised Biography of T. E. Lawrence* (London: Heinemann, 1989).

Wilson, Jeremy, *T. E. Lawrence* (London: National Portrait Gallery, 1989).

Yardley, Michael, *Backing into the Limelight: A Biography of T. E. Lawrence* (London: Harrap, 1985).

About the Film

Bogarde, Dirk, *Snakes and Ladders* (London: Chatto & Windus, 1978).

Brownlow, Kevin, *David Lean* (London: Faber, 1996; republished 1997).

Caton, Steven C., *Lawrence of Arabia: A Film's Anthropology* (Berkeley: University of California Press, 1999).

Hayman, Ronald, *Robert Bolt* (London: Heinemann, 1969).

Kelly, Andrew, Jeffrey Richards and James Pepper, *Filming T. E. Lawrence: Korda's Lost Epics* (London: I. B. Tauris, 1997).

Kent, Howard, *Single Bed for Three: A Lawrence of Arabia Notebook* (London: Hutchinson, 1963).

Lean, Sandra, with Barry Chattington, *David Lean: An Intimate Portrait* (New York: Universe, 2001).

Morris, L. Robert and Lawrence Raskin, *Lawrence of Arabia: The 30th Anniversary Pictorial History* (New York: Doubleday, 1992).

Sinclair, Andrew, *Spiegel: The Man Behind the Pictures* (London: Hamish Hamilton, 1987).

Turner, Adrian, *The Making of Lawrence of Arabia* (Limpsfield, Surrey: Dragon's World, 1994).

Turner, Adrian, *Robert Bolt: Scenes from Two Lives* (London: Hutchinson, 1998).

Wilcox, Herbert, *Twenty-five Thousand Sunsets* (London: Bodley Head, 1967).